Certification Study Companion Series

The Apress Certification Study Companion Series offers guidance and hands-on practice to support technical and business professionals who are studying for an exam in the pursuit of an industry certification. Professionals worldwide seek to achieve certifications in order to advance in a career role, reinforce knowledge in a specific discipline, or to apply for or change jobs. This series focuses on the most widely taken certification exams in a given field. It is designed to be user friendly, tracking to topics as they appear in a given exam and work alongside other certification material as professionals prepare for their exam.

More information about this series at https://link.springer.com/bookseries/17100.

Microsoft Power Platform Solution Architect Certification Companion

Mastering the PL-600 Certification

Loganathan K

Apress®

Microsoft Power Platform Solution Architect Certification Companion: Mastering the PL-600 Certification

Loganathan K
Bangalore, Karnataka, India

ISBN-13 (pbk): 979-8-8688-1509-6 ISBN-13 (electronic): 979-8-8688-1510-2
https://doi.org/10.1007/979-8-8688-1510-2

Copyright © 2025 by Loganathan K

This work is subject to copyright. All rights are reserved by the Publisher, whether the whole or part of the material is concerned, specifically the rights of translation, reprinting, reuse of illustrations, recitation, broadcasting, reproduction on microfilms or in any other physical way, and transmission or information storage and retrieval, electronic adaptation, computer software, or by similar or dissimilar methodology now known or hereafter developed.

Trademarked names, logos, and images may appear in this book. Rather than use a trademark symbol with every occurrence of a trademarked name, logo, or image we use the names, logos, and images only in an editorial fashion and to the benefit of the trademark owner, with no intention of infringement of the trademark.

The use in this publication of trade names, trademarks, service marks, and similar terms, even if they are not identified as such, is not to be taken as an expression of opinion as to whether or not they are subject to proprietary rights.

While the advice and information in this book are believed to be true and accurate at the date of publication, neither the authors nor the editors nor the publisher can accept any legal responsibility for any errors or omissions that may be made. The publisher makes no warranty, express or implied, with respect to the material contained herein.

Managing Director, Apress Media LLC: Welmoed Spahr
Acquisitions Editor: Smriti Srivastava
Development Editor: Laura Berendson
Editorial Assistant: Jessica Vakili

Cover designed by eStudioCalamar

Distributed to the book trade worldwide by Springer Science+Business Media New York, 1 New York Plaza, New York, NY 10004. Phone 1-800-SPRINGER, fax (201) 348-4505, e-mail orders-ny@springer-sbm.com, or visit www.springeronline.com. Apress Media, LLC is a Delaware LLC and the sole member (owner) is Springer Science + Business Media Finance Inc (SSBM Finance Inc). SSBM Finance Inc is a **Delaware** corporation.

For information on translations, please e-mail booktranslations@springernature.com; for reprint, paperback, or audio rights, please e-mail bookpermissions@springernature.com.

Apress titles may be purchased in bulk for academic, corporate, or promotional use. eBook versions and licenses are also available for most titles. For more information, reference our Print and eBook Bulk Sales web page at http://www.apress.com/bulk-sales.

Any source code or other supplementary material referenced by the author in this book is available to readers on GitHub. For more detailed information, please visit https://www.apress.com/gp/services/source-code.

If disposing of this product, please recycle the paper

I dedicate this book to my beloved wife, Kousalya, whose unwavering support, patience, and belief in me have been my greatest source of strength. Her encouragement kept me going through challenges and countless late-night study sessions. I am especially grateful for her valuable support in language refinement and clarity, which helped shape this work into what it is today.

Next, I express my deepest gratitude to my parents, Kalamani Kandhasamy and K S Kandhasamy, and my elder brothers, K Suresh and K Prakash. Their sacrifices, love, and guidance have shaped my journey and are the very foundation of who I am today.

This book is a tribute to all of you. Thank you for being a part of my journey.

Table of Contents

About the Author xix

About the Technical Reviewer xxi

Acknowledgments xxiii

Introduction xxv

Chapter 1: Getting Started with the PL-600 Exam: Overview and Essentials 1
    1. Introduction 2
    2. Prerequisites 2
    3. Domains and Skills 3
        Key Skills You'll Need 4
    4. How to Prepare for the Exam 5
        Planning 6
        Preparation 6
        Instructor-Led Training 7
        Practice Exam 7
    5. Exam Accommodations 8
        Ensure Name Consistency 8
        Prepare Attachments 9
        Send Request Email 9
        Validity Period 9

TABLE OF CONTENTS

    Exam Schedule Process with ESL 10
    Reasons for Application Rejection 10
    Other Than ESL Accommodations 10
  6. Steps to Register for the PL-600 Exam 11
    Set Up Your Microsoft Learn Account 11
    Why Personal Email? 12
    Steps to Follow Before the Exam 14
    Tips for a Successful System Check 15
  7. Microsoft Exam Structure and Format 16
    1. Case Studies 17
    2. Question Series 17
    3. Multiple Choice (Single Answer) 17
    4. Multiple Choice (Multiple Answers) 18
    5. Drag and Drop 18
    6. Hot Area 18
    7. Build List 18
    8. Lab Simulations 19
    9. Scenario-Based Questions 19
    10. True/False 19
    11. Inline Choice 19
  8. Key Points to Remember During the Exam 20
    Time Management 20
    Exam Room Requirements 21
  Conclusion 21

Chapter 2: Building a Successful Solution Architect Framework: Key Stages and Skills 23
  Introduction 24
  The Path to Becoming a Solution Architect 24

Technologies Every Solution Architect Should Know	26
Key Soft Skills for a Solution Architect: 6 C's	29
Solution Architect Role in a Project	**31**
Presales	31
Initiation	32
Analysis and Design	32
Implementation	33
Delivery	34
Operation	34
Pillars of a Great Architecture for Business Applications	**35**
1. Security	35
2. Empowering End Users	36
3. Trust and Privacy	37
4. Maintainability	38
5. Availability and Recoverability	38
6. Performance and Scalability	39
7. Efficiency and Operations	40
8. Shared Responsibility	40
9. Design Choices and Trade-offs	41
Summary	42
Customer Discovery Essentials for a Solution Architect	**43**
Introduction	43
Key Topics Covered in Customer Discovery	43
Initial Customer Discovery: The Process	45
Discovery Meetings	47
Customer Communication Strategy for Solution Architects	48
Summary	52

TABLE OF CONTENTS

Crafting and Proposing Effective Solutions 53
Introduction 53
A Structured Approach for Solution Architects 53
Identifying and Proposing Solution Components: A Presales Approach 59
1. Mapping Customer Needs to Functionality 59
2. Customization vs. Out-of-the-Box Solutions 60
3. Solution Blueprint Documentation 60
4. User Experience and Wireframes 61
5. Process and Data Modeling 61
6. Identifying Third-Party Components 61
7. Integration with Existing Systems 62
8. Deployment Options 62
9. Next Steps and Solution Refinement 62
Develop and Validate a Demo 63
Solution Architect Involvement 65
Keep or Discard 65
Manage Expectations 66
Identifying Potential Third-Party Components for Your Solution 66
Evaluating the ISV (Independent Software Vendor) 67
Evaluating Licensing 69
Recognizing Strengths and Weaknesses in a Solution 70
Summary 74
Effective Requirement Gathering: From Functional to Nonfunctional Needs 75
Introduction 75
Leading Requirement Capture Sessions 75
What a Requirement Looks Like 76
Driving Toward Requirement Clarity 78
Resolving Conflicting Requirements 78

Standing Up for Your Perspective 78
Identifying Functional Requirements 79
Poorly Worded Requirements 79
Mapping to Process 80
Acceptance Criteria 80
Capture Exceptions 81
Avoiding Scope Creep 81
Identifying Nonfunctional Requirements 82
Feasibility of Nonfunctional Requirements 85
Finalizing Requirements: A Step-by-Step Review Process 86
Additional Considerations for Finalizing Requirements 89

Assessing and Refining Requirements 90
Introduction to Fit-Gap Analysis 90
Determining the Feasibility of Requirements 90
Learn from a Proof of Concept (PoC) 93
Categorizing Business Requirements and Performing Fit-Gap Analysis 95
Evaluate Dynamics 365 and Microsoft Power Platform Apps 97
Connectors and APIs 97
Industry Accelerators and Common Data Model 97
AppSource 98
Summary 99

Conclusion: Building a Successful Solution Architect Framework 100

Chapter 3: Governance, Architecture, and Core Components in Power Platform and Dynamics 365 101

Introduction 102
Project Governance in Power Platform and Dynamics 365 102
Introduction to Project Governance 102
Keeping Projects on Track 103

TABLE OF CONTENTS

    Project Governance: A Guide for Solution Architects 103
        The Essentials of Governance 105
        Reflecting on Your Experience 105
        Solution Architect's Role in Project Governance...............................106
        Defining Governance with Microsoft Power Platform.......................106
    Power Platform Architecture 112
        Introduction 112
        Microsoft Power Platform Components..112
        Microsoft Power Platform Capabilities 114
        The Role of Data 115
        Accessing Dataverse Through Environments 115
        Custom Logic in Microsoft Dataverse...126
        Design Considerations..130
        Platform Limits in Microsoft Power Platform 131
        High Availability and Disaster Recovery Considerations for Microsoft Power Platform Solutions..135
    Exploring Power Apps and Automate 140
        Introduction to Power Apps 140
        Microsoft Apps vs. Partner Apps vs. Custom Apps 141
        Choosing the Right App Type 142
        Extending Existing Apps vs. Creating New Ones 144
        Components in Power Apps: Enhancing Reusability and Collaboration........146
        Types of Components in Power Apps 146
        Managing Components: Best Practices 148
        Optimizing Canvas Apps: Techniques for Better Performance and User Experience..148
        Techniques for Optimizing Canvas Apps...149
        Tools for Monitoring and Testing Canvas Apps 151

TABLE OF CONTENTS

Microsoft Teams and Power Apps: A Seamless Collaboration for Teams 153

Power Apps Portals: Exposing Dataverse Data to Internal and External Audiences 156

Automation Options for Solution Architects in Power Automate 161

Assessing the Cost of Automation 166

Triggers in Power Automate 166

Common Actions in Power Automate (with Dataverse Connector).............170

Business Process Flows in Power Automate and Power Platform 175

Conclusion 179

Chapter 4: Leveraging Microsoft Copilot and RPA and Securing Data Models in Power Platform Solutions 181

Introduction 182

Robotic Process Automation (RPA) Overview 183

    Challenges with Legacy Systems 183

    The Power of Automation with Power Automate 183

    Role of a Solution Architect 184

    Best Practices for Designing Flows 185

    Power Automate for Desktop 186

    Deployment and IT Coordination 187

    Browser Requirements 188

    Integration with Microsoft Power Platform 188

    Solutions and Application Lifecycle Management (ALM) 188

    Record and Edit Tasks in Power Automate for Desktop 189

    Variables in Desktop Flows 191

    Running Desktop Flows 192

    Virtual Machines for Unattended Flows 193

    Process Mining in Power Automate 194

TABLE OF CONTENTS

Introduction to Microsoft Copilot Studio and Agents 196
    The Challenges of Building Agents 197
    Microsoft Copilot Studio 198
    Use Cases for Agents 198
    Solution Architect's Role in Deploying Agents 200
    Responsible AI Principles 201
    Agent Building Options: Choosing the Right Approach 202
    Key Concepts for Building Agents 205

Data Modeling and Security for Power Platform Solutions 210
    Introduction 210
    Common Data Model – A Solution Architect's Essential Tool for Data Interoperability 212
    Key Features of the Common Data Model 213
    Industry Accelerators in Microsoft's Ecosystem 215
    Benefits of Common Data Model 216
    Data Modeling in Microsoft Power Platform: Designing Effective Data Architectures 217
    Types of Data Models 217
    Entity Relationship Diagrams (ERDs) 219
    Object Diagrams 219
    Data Modeling Strategies 220
    Factors Influencing Data Models 221
    Choosing the Right Data Store for Your Microsoft Power Platform Apps 222
    Data Stores in Microsoft Power Platform 222
    Choosing Where to Store Data 227
    Data Model: Environment Security 228
    Microsoft Entra ID Authentication 228
    Security Groups and Environment Access 231

Roles and Administration	231
Data Loss Prevention (DLP)	232
Access to Dataverse	235
Security in Apps: A Solution Architect's Perspective	241
Conclusion	245

Chapter 5: Implementing Analytics, AI, and ALM Strategies for Power Platform Success 247

Assessing and Implementing Analytics, AI, and Integration Strategies, ALM in Power Platform 248
    Introduction 248

Analytics and Reporting 249
    Introduction 249
    The Solution Architect's Role in Reporting and Analytics 249
    Types of Reporting and Analytics 250
    Prebuilt Insights in Microsoft Dynamics 365 251
    Key Questions for Solution Architects 252
    Leveraging AI for Reporting and Analytics 253
    Power Platform Reporting Capabilities 254
    Alternative Reporting Options 258

Artificial Intelligence 259
    Dynamics 365 AI Apps 260
    Azure Cognitive Services 260
    OpenAI Integration 260
    Azure Machine Learning 261
    AI Builder 261
    Integration with Power Platform 261
    Choosing the Right AI Solution 262

TABLE OF CONTENTS

Integration in Power Platform: The Solution Architect's Role 262
- What Is Integration? 262
- Why Is Integration Necessary? 263
- Types of Integration 264
- How Solution Architects Help with Integration 265
- Integration Challenges in Power Platform: Overcoming the Hurdles 267
- Influencers of Integration Design 268
- Causes of Integration Failures 269
- Designing for Resilience 270
- The Integration Design Process 271
- Categorizing Data for Integration 272

Application Lifecycle Management and Go-Live Strategies 273
- Introduction 273
- Application Lifecycle Management with Microsoft Power Platform 274
- Microsoft's Vision for ALM 274
- The Solution Architect's Role in ALM 275
- Solutions in Microsoft Power Platform 276
- Types of Solutions 277
- Solution Layering 277
- Strategies for Solution Structure 278
- Rules for Creating Solutions 279
- Solution Splitting: Horizontal and Vertical Approaches 279
- ALM with Azure DevOps for Microsoft Power Platform 280
- Pipelines in Power Platform 281
- Deployment Methodologies in Azure DevOps 282
- Go-Live Plan for Solution Deployment 283

Conclusion 290

TABLE OF CONTENTS

Chapter 6: Assessing Your Expertise As a Microsoft Power Platform Solution Architect 291

Introduction 292

Case Study No. 1 292

Use Case: Leveraging Power Platform Components in a Real-World Apparel Manufacturing 292

1. Power Apps: Canvas App for Data Capture 294

2. Power Automate: Automated Report Submission and Alerts ... 294

3. Power BI: Real-Time Data Dashboards and KPI Monitoring 295

Outcome 296

Case Study No. 2 297

Digitizing Training School Processes with Microsoft Power Platform 297

Power Platform Components 298

Takeaways 300

Case Study No. 3 300

Transforming E-Commerce Operations with Microsoft Power Platform 300

Core Components of a Power Platform E-Commerce Solution 301

Step-by-Step Implementation Plan 303

Benefits for Small Garment Companies 304

Case Study No. 4 305

Maximize Compliance: Self-Assessments and Audits with Power Platform 305

Creating an Assessment and Auditing System Using Power Platform 306

Benefits of Power Platform for Compliance and Technical Auditing 310

Case Study No. 5 310

Transform Vendor Evaluation with Power Platform 310

Evaluation Criteria 311

Use Case 312

xvii

TABLE OF CONTENTS

SQL Data Modeling 314
Power BI Dashboard and Report 315
Case Study No. 6 316
Bridging Skill Gaps in Apparel Production Using Power Platform Tools 316
Proposed Solution 317
Benefits 319
Case Study No. 7 319
Bridging Skill Gaps: Leveraging Power Platform for Production Line Expansion and Attrition 319
Power BI Dashboard for Management 321
Scheduled Alerts and Real-Time Decision-Making 322
Conclusion 323

Index **325**

About the Author

Loganathan K is a seasoned Microsoft Certified Trainer (MCT) and Functional Consultant with expertise in Microsoft Power Platform, Dynamics 365, and business process automation. With a career spanning the apparel manufacturing industry and IT consulting, he has a proven track record of leading QMS development, training programs, and compliance audits, managing large-scale operations with 4,000+ employees, and overseeing multiple digital transformation projects. His passion for teaching and mentoring has led him to train college faculties, industry professionals, and students on Microsoft technologies, helping them gain certifications and career advancements. As an active content creator, Loganathan shares insights on Power Platform, Dynamics 365, and automation solutions through his blog, *LK Techs*, LinkedIn posts, and YouTube videos.

With *Microsoft Power Platform Solution Architect Certification Companion: Mastering the PL-600 Certification*, Loganathan brings his real-world experience, practical insights, and solution architecture knowledge to help aspiring consultants and solution architects confidently tackle the PL-600 exam and build robust digital solutions.

About the Technical Reviewer

Mittal Mehta is a seasoned technologist with expertise in Artificial Intelligence, DevSecOps automation, configuration, and release management for both on-premises and cloud applications. He is passionate when it comes to learning new technologies in AI, automation, and cloud security. Mittal has extensive experience with Microsoft technologies such as C#, Azure, PowerShell, and DevOps. Currently, he serves as a Principal Consultant in AI and automation in Bangalore, India, specializing in cloud automation and Azure DevOps processes. He has also reviewed numerous books on Azure DevOps, Git, security, release management, and Artificial Intelligence.

Acknowledgments

I would like to extend my heartfelt thanks to my mentors and friends—Bharath Jeyaraj https://www.linkedin.com/in/bharath-jeyaraj-45071628/, Santhosh V https://www.linkedin.com/in/santhosh-v-250993a0/, Rebecca Nanthakumar https://www.linkedin.com/in/rebecca-herbert-4406ba236/, Nanthakumar G K https://www.linkedin.com/in/nanthakumar-g-k-90796945/, Rameshkumar L https://www.linkedin.com/in/ramesh-kumar-71735632/, Ravi Kumar C V, Thangavel K https://www.linkedin.com/in/thangavel-k-a3721296/, Kamalendu Sith https://www.linkedin.com/in/kamalendu-sith-4a4908a/, and Praveena Saravanan https://www.linkedin.com/in/praveena-saravanan/—for their invaluable contributions and guidance. Their wisdom and support have played a pivotal role in my professional growth.

Special thanks to Gomathi Srinivasan https://www.linkedin.com/in/gomathisri/, Microsoft MVP and MCT community lead, for her continuous guidance, encouragement, and invaluable contributions to the MCT community, which have greatly inspired me. I also thank Praveena, a UI/UX designer.

I would like to extend my gratitude to the top management of Atna Technologies India Pvt Ltd https://www.linkedin.com/company/atna-technologies-india-pvt-ltd/—Gopalakrishnan S https://www.linkedin.com/in/gopalakrishnan-s-a194895/, Srividhya https://www.linkedin.com/in/srividhya-subramony-a4b38a4/, Rajesh K P https://www.linkedin.com/in/rajesh-kp-406334235/, and Ravindranathan T https://www.linkedin.com/in/ravindranathan-t-b5884419/—for their support and guidance on my professional journey.

Introduction

This PL-600 Exam Companion is designed to be your ultimate guide for mastering the skills required to become a Microsoft Power Platform Solution Architect. Whether you are an aspiring solution architect, a consultant, or an experienced professional looking to validate your expertise, this book provides a structured approach to help you succeed in the Microsoft PL-600 certification exam.

Why This Book?

The role of a Power Platform Solution Architect is critical in designing, implementing, and governing solutions that align with business and technical needs. This exam evaluates your ability to lead solution design, ensure quality, and manage stakeholder expectations. This book is tailored to

- Provide a comprehensive breakdown of PL-600 exam objectives
- Offer real-world scenarios and best practices to bridge theoretical knowledge with practical implementation
- Include exam tips, practice questions, and case studies to enhance understanding and retention

INTRODUCTION

Who Should Use This Book?

This book is ideal for

- Solution architects designing and leading Power Platform solutions
- Functional consultants and developers aiming to transition into an architecture role
- IT professionals and business analysts involved in digital transformation projects
- Anyone preparing for the PL-600 Microsoft Power Platform Solution Architect certification exam

How to Use This Book

Each chapter aligns with the exam syllabus and is structured to help you

1. Understand key concepts with clear explanations and examples
2. Apply knowledge through case studies and real-world scenarios
3. Assess your readiness with practice questions and exam tips

Final Thoughts

The journey to becoming a Power Platform Solution Architect requires both technical expertise and strategic vision. This book will serve as your trusted companion in building the knowledge and confidence needed to excel in the PL-600 exam and in real-world solution design.

Let's begin your journey toward success!

CHAPTER 1

Getting Started with the PL-600 Exam: Overview and Essentials

Chapter Goal: The goal of this chapter is to provide a clear overview of the PL-600 exam, its key objectives, and practical preparation strategies for certification success.

Sub-topics:

1. Introduction to the PL-600 Exam
2. Eligibility and Prerequisites
3. Key Skills and Domains Covered
4. How to Prepare for the Exam
5. Exam Accommodations
6. Steps to Register for the PL-600 Exam
7. Exam Structure and Format
8. Key Points to Remember During the Exam

CHAPTER 1   GETTING STARTED WITH THE PL-600 EXAM: OVERVIEW AND ESSENTIALS

1. Introduction

Hello, and welcome! If you're here, it's likely because you're considering—or have already decided—to become a Certified Microsoft Power Platform Solution Architect.

In this book, I'll walk you through everything you need to know to pass the PL-600 exam with confidence. We'll discuss why this certification matters, the skills you need to develop, and the steps you should take to ensure success. By the end, you'll feel fully prepared to take on the challenge!

2. Prerequisites

Before we jump into the prep work, let's talk about whether you're ready for this journey. PL-600 isn't your typical entry-level exam. Already you have some hands-on experience with the Power Platform—such as Power Apps, Power Automate, Power BI—or with Dynamics 365 and its related components.

Think of the exam as the finishing touch on a strong foundation of experience. Most candidates have been functional consultants, senior developers, or even project managers. If you're comfortable solving business challenges with technology, you're in the right place. We'll build on what you know and dive deeper into key areas like architecture, integration, and governance.

If you're already certified as a Power Platform Functional Consultant (PL-200) or Power Platform Developer Associate (PL-400), it can give you an edge in preparing for the PL-600 certification. While having these certifications is an added advantage, it's not a mandatory requirement. But don't worry—if you're relatively new, I'll guide you on where to start. You can still successfully tackle PL-600 without them—this book will guide you through everything you need.

3. Domains and Skills

This is where we get to the heart of PL-600. The exam focuses on turning business requirements into scalable solutions. Sounds fancy, right? But really, it's all about making sure an organization's Power Platform solutions meet both business and technical needs.

As a candidate for the PL-600 exam, it's important to have experience in solution architecture across both functional and technical areas of Microsoft Power Platform. You'll need to be comfortable making design decisions based on best practices in areas like development, configuration, integration, infrastructure, security, licensing, storage, and change management.

In this role, your main responsibility will be to architect and implement comprehensive end-to-end solutions that meet both business and technical needs. You'll need a good grasp of

- Microsoft Power Platform
- Dynamics 365 customer engagement apps
- Related Microsoft cloud solutions
- Third-party technologies

It's also beneficial to be familiar with the Power Platform Well-Architected Framework, ideally having used it in previous implementations.

CHAPTER 1   GETTING STARTED WITH THE PL-600 EXAM: OVERVIEW AND ESSENTIALS

Key Skills You'll Need

Solution Envisioning and Requirement Analysis (45–50%)

This involves understanding the business needs and planning a solution that aligns with Organization/Business Process requirements. You'll gather and refine both high-level and detailed requirements, identify the necessary Microsoft Power Platform solution components, and perform fit/gap analyses. This ensures that the proposed solution meets the business's functional and nonfunctional requirements while identifying any gaps and alternative approaches using existing apps, Dynamics 365, AppSource apps, or third-party components.

Architecting the Solution (35–40%)

In this phase, you lead the design process. This includes defining the solution's architecture and topology and designing data models, security models, and integrations. You'll decide how data should be migrated and integrated with other systems and how the solution fits into the broader technical environment. This step requires careful planning of data automation strategies and visualization strategies and ensuring the environment's infrastructure is ready to support the solution.

Implementing the Solution (15–20%)

Once the design is finalized, it's time to ensure the solution is properly implemented. This includes validating the design to ensure it meets security standards, follows business rules, and adheres to API limits. You'll troubleshoot issues related to performance, integrations, or automations and ensure the solution is ready for deployment. As go-live approaches, you'll monitor the solution's performance, resolve any remaining issues, and ensure all components work smoothly in a live environment.

CHAPTER 1   GETTING STARTED WITH THE PL-600 EXAM: OVERVIEW AND ESSENTIALS

(As of December 2024, the skills required for the PL-600 exam may be updated. While this book covers the current key areas, the exam's scope is subject to change, so it's essential to check for the latest requirements on Microsoft Learn to ensure you're fully prepared.)

4. How to Prepare for the Exam

Alright, now let's dive into the fun part—preparing for the PL-600 exam! There are plenty of resources available to help you ace this certification, and I'm excited to share some of the best. First and foremost, Microsoft Learn is an absolute goldmine. It offers guided learning paths completely free of charge, so if you haven't explored it yet, I highly encourage you to do so. But before we get started, I want to make sure you have your own Microsoft Learn account. If you don't have one yet, let's create it!

As you create your account, keep a few tips in mind:

- First, use a personal email address that you check regularly to avoid missing important updates or verification emails from Microsoft.

- You can link up to five other accounts, such as your organizational or institutional email, to your Microsoft Learn account. This feature allows you to seamlessly access and share resources, collaborate with colleagues or classmates, and enhance your learning experience by leveraging multiple account.

- You can link your LinkedIn account to your Microsoft Learn profile, allowing you to showcase your achievements as an online verifiable link. This feature makes it easy to share your completed courses and certifications with potential employers or colleagues, enhancing your professional profile and demonstrating your commitment to continuous learning.

CHAPTER 1   GETTING STARTED WITH THE PL-600 EXAM: OVERVIEW AND ESSENTIALS

I hope you've successfully created your Microsoft Learn account! Now, let's dive into how to make the most of self-learning on the platform. I'd like to share my personal approach to exam preparation, which has really helped me stay organized and motivated throughout my learning journey.

Planning

The very first step before taking any exam is to establish a timeline. I recommend keeping this timeframe short; it creates a sense of urgency that motivates you to prepare effectively and prevents the preparation process from dragging on.

Preparation

Before diving into my studies, I create an Excel file where I list all the Microsoft Learn modules relevant to the exam. This serves as a comprehensive planner, making it easier to track my progress. I ensure that my planner is realistic and achievable, including time for practice exams as part of my preparation.

Additionally, I schedule the exam before I start studying. This commitment helps me stay focused and gives me a clear target to work toward, ultimately driving me to stick to my planner and achieve my goals.

In the event of any delays, Microsoft allows you to reschedule your exam for a more convenient date. It's a good idea to keep an alternative date in mind, but be sure not to rely on that backup date for your preparation timeline. Stay focused on your original schedule to maintain motivation and ensure you're fully prepared for the exam.

> *"Effective planning and thorough preparation are the keys to achieving anything."*

Instructor-Led Training

I also recommend considering instructor-led courses if you prefer a classroom learning environment, especially when your budget allows and your time is limited. These courses provide the opportunity to ask questions and delve deeper into specific topics. Typically, after completing an instructor-led course. Usually lasting four to five days, depending on the training institute, you'll gain valuable insights into the certification process. While these courses can help prepare you for the exam, it's essential to supplement your learning by studying the Microsoft Learn modules. This combination will give you a comprehensive understanding of the related content and ensure you're well-prepared for the certification.

Practice Exam

Don't forget to take advantage of the practice exams available on Microsoft Learn. These exams consist of 50 multiple-choice questions, and you'll need to score at least 80% to pass. They are an excellent way to identify your weaker areas and boost your confidence before the actual exam. By reviewing your results, you can focus your study efforts on the topics that need improvement, ensuring you're better prepared when the time comes to take the exam. You can access the practice exam through the PL-600 Microsoft Certification Learn page, where it is listed as "Take a free practice assessment" under schedule exam (Figure 1-1).

CHAPTER 1   GETTING STARTED WITH THE PL-600 EXAM: OVERVIEW AND ESSENTIALS

Figure 1-1. *"Take a free practice assessment" from Microsoft Learn*

5. Exam Accommodations

Below are the steps to apply for ESL accommodation for a Microsoft certification exam

Ensure Name Consistency

- Your name must be consistent across the next documents:
    - Government-issued ID proof (e.g., passport, driver's license, PAN card)
    - MS Learn Account profile name
    - ESL Form: Includes your name, MS Learn details (name, ID, etc.)
    - Employer Acknowledgment Letter: Must be on official letterhead with the employer's signature

Prepare Attachments

- ESL Form
- Employer Acknowledgment Letter

Send Request Email

- Use your MS Learn login email address to send the request email.
- Include the following attachments:
  - ESL Form
  - Employer Acknowledgment Letter (students can collect from institutions)
- Email Subject: ESL Application Request – [Your Full Name]
- Mail ID: AccommodationsPearsonVUE@pearson.com

Validity Period

- The ESL accommodation, once approved, is valid for two years from the date of approval.
- This extended time allows candidates to use Pearson's exam features, like accessing MS Learn content and reviewing answers.

CHAPTER 1   GETTING STARTED WITH THE PL-600 EXAM: OVERVIEW AND ESSENTIALS

Exam Schedule Process with ESL

After your ESL accommodation is approved, you will get an email with detailed instructions on how to schedule your exam. Please note that the exam scheduling must be done over the phone, not online.

Reasons for Application Rejection

Make sure that your name matches exactly across all documents—MS Learn Account, government ID, ESL Form, and Acknowledgment Letter. Any discrepancies lead to delays or rejection, so verifying this in advance will save time and avoid complications.

Other Than ESL Accommodations

Microsoft ensures everyone has a fair chance to succeed by offering accommodations for their certification exams. These include

1. Extra time for those with processing or learning difficulties
2. Assistive tools like screen readers, magnifiers, or voice recognition software
3. Breaks for medical needs or conditions like anxiety
4. Quiet environments for better focus
5. Physical accessibility, like wheelchair-friendly setups or adjustable desks
6. Custom exam formats such as Braille or large print for visual impairments
7. Interpreters for sign language needs

CHAPTER 1   GETTING STARTED WITH THE PL-600 EXAM: OVERVIEW AND ESSENTIALS

Medical items like snacks or devices are allowed in the test room.

Requesting accommodations is straightforward—submit your need with supporting documents, and Microsoft takes care of the rest. With these in place, you can focus on showcasing your skills!

Click Accommodation or scan QR (Figure 1-2) or search Microsoft Exam Accommodation in the browser.

Figure 1-2. For more information about Microsoft exam accommodations

6. Steps to Register for the PL-600 Exam

Let's see how to apply for the Microsoft PL-600 exam in the following steps.

Before we get into the actual application process, let me reiterate something important from the "How to Prepare for the Exam" section—because this step is crucial to ensure a smooth journey ahead.

Set Up Your Microsoft Learn Account

Make sure you've created a **Microsoft Learn account** using a personal email address, such as @outlook.com or @hotmail.com. If you don't already have one, take a moment to create it.

CHAPTER 1   GETTING STARTED WITH THE PL-600 EXAM: OVERVIEW AND ESSENTIALS

Why Personal Email?

Using your office or school email might seem fine now, but you risk losing access if you ever leave your organization or institution. A personal email ensures you always have full control of your account. Microsoft Learn accounts allow you to link up to five organizational or school email IDs later, so you'll still have the flexibility to connect it with work or school accounts if needed.

Once you've created your Microsoft Learn account, it's time to apply for the PL-600 exam. You've got a few easy options to get started:

1. **Using a Web Browser**

   Open your browser and search for **"PL-600 Power Platform Solution Architect Exam."** Click on one of the official Microsoft links, and you'll find all the details you need to register.

2. **On Your Smartphone or Tablet**

   Got an Android or Apple device? Just scan the QR code shown in Figure 1-3, and it'll take you straight to the exam application page.

Figure 1-3. For more information about Microsoft Power Platform Solution Architect Certification

CHAPTER 1   GETTING STARTED WITH THE PL-600 EXAM: OVERVIEW AND ESSENTIALS

3. **If You're Reading This Online**

   For those using the online version of this book, it's even simpler—just click the link below to apply: PL-600 Power Platform Solution Architect Exam.

The methods mentioned above will take you directly to the PL-600 certification page. Once you're there, scroll down until you see a section like the one shown in Figure 1-4. Click **"Schedule exam"** to choose your preferred method: online or test center.

Figure 1-4. Exam Scheduling from Microsoft Learn

Before deciding, here are a couple of things to consider:

1. **Internet Connection:** Do you have a stable Internet connection at home with no connectivity issues?

2. **Quiet Environment:** Do you have a private space where no one will disturb you for at least two hours?

If your answer is **Yes** to both, the Online Exam option is the most convenient. You can take it right from the comfort of your home.

If your answer is **No**, it's better to schedule your exam at a nearby test center, where you can focus and complete the exam without distractions.

13

Once you've selected your preferred method—online or test center—here's what to do next:

1. **Confirm Your Preferred Language**

   Make sure you choose the language you're most comfortable with for the exam.

2. **Verify Your Name**

   Double-check that the name on your profile matches exactly with your government ID. This is super important, as any mismatch could cause issues on exam day.

3. **Pick a Convenient Time**

   Browse through the available slots, choose a time that works best for you, and lock it in.

Lastly, if you have a discount voucher, don't forget to apply it during checkout to save some money!

Steps to Follow Before the Exam

If you've chosen the Online Exam option, there's one more important step to complete before exam day: a **system check**.

Here's How It Works

After applying, you'll receive a confirmation email from the exam provider (Figure 1-5). In that email, you'll find instructions for performing a system check—it's a mandatory step to ensure everything runs smoothly.

CHAPTER 1   GETTING STARTED WITH THE PL-600 EXAM: OVERVIEW AND ESSENTIALS

Microsoft Certification Exam:	PL-600 - Microsoft Power Platform Solution Architect - English (ENU)
Candidate:	
Candidate ID:	
Registration ID:	
Date	Sunday, December 29, 2024
Time:	06:45 PM India Standard Time
Appointment Length (Includes time to review the Candidate Agreement, instructions and tutorial, answer the exam questions, and provide comments; if the exam does not include labs, the time will be 20 minutes less than this by design)	150 Minutes
System test:	Test your system
Exam check-in:	Check in to start exam
	Check-in begins 30 minutes prior to the appointment time or, sign into your candidate website.

Figure 1-5. *Mail screenshot for your reference: Test your system*

Tips for a Successful System Check

1. Use the **same computer** you plan to use for the exam.

2. Connect to the **same Internet network** you'll rely on during the exam.

3. Perform the check in the **exact same location** where you'll take the test.

If you need to change your exam setup (place or network) closer to the exam, make sure to redo the system check.

How to manage exam from a Microsoft Learn account?

You can easily manage your exam appointment through your **Microsoft Learn account**. Here's how.

Go to **Profile ➤ Credentials ➤ Certifications**, where you'll find all the details for your PL-600 exam. From this section, you can (Figure 1-6)

- **Test your system** ahead of the exam
- **Check in on exam day** to start the process
- **Reschedule or cancel** your exam if needed

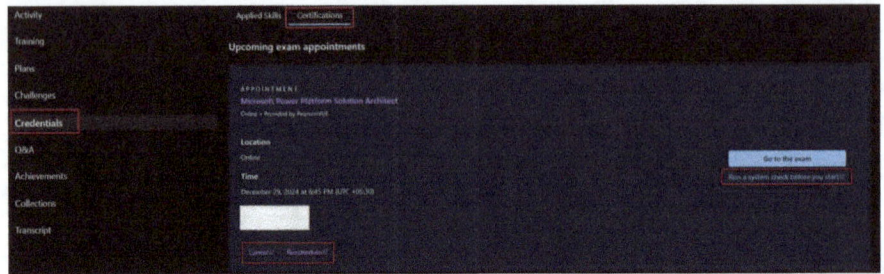

Figure 1-6. *System Test from Your Microsoft Learn Account before Exam*

Important Notes

- If you need to **reschedule**, make sure you do it at least 24 hours before your appointment. There's no limit on how many times you can reschedule.

- On **exam day**, log in **30 minutes early** to complete essential checks like
  - Verifying your system
  - Confirming your ID
  - Ensuring your test space meets the requirements

Being prepared with these steps will make your exam day smooth and stress-free!

7. Microsoft Exam Structure and Format

When preparing for the PL-600 Microsoft Power Platform Solution Architect certification, understanding the exam structure and question formats can help you perform confidently and effectively.

Let's dive into the types of questions you might encounter during the exam.

CHAPTER 1   GETTING STARTED WITH THE PL-600 EXAM: OVERVIEW AND ESSENTIALS

1. Case Studies

Imagine you're a solution architect tasked with designing a Power Platform solution for a complex business scenario. In the exam, you'll be given detailed case studies outlining requirements, challenges, and goals. You'll analyze these scenarios and propose the best solutions, showcasing your ability to address real-world business needs.

Example:
The case study might describe a company needing to automate approval processes across departments using Power Automate while ensuring sensitive data is secured via Dataverse roles.

2. Question Series

These are sets of questions centered around a specific area, such as solution design or deployment. The questions might require multiple-choice answers, drag-and-drop matching, or step-by-step task completion.

3. Multiple Choice (Single Answer)

A classic format where you select one correct answer from the provided options. These questions test your foundational knowledge, like choosing the correct Dataverse table type for storing hierarchical data.

Example:
Which table type in Dataverse is optimized for storing hierarchical relationships?

    A. Standard Table

    B. Activity Table

    C. Lookup Table

    D. Custom Table

4. Multiple Choice (Multiple Answers)

These questions require selecting two or more correct options. The question will specify how many answers to choose.

Example:
Which two components are necessary for setting up security in a Power Platform solution?

    A.   Security Roles

    B.   Environment Variables

    C.   Field-Level Permissions

    D.   Power BI Dashboard

5. Drag and Drop

This format tests your ability to logically sequence steps or match items to categories. You might need to arrange steps for configuring Dataverse or match Power Platform components to their respective use cases.

6. Hot Area

You'll interact with an image or diagram and click on the area that corresponds to the correct answer. For example, you might be shown a screen from the Power Platform admin center and asked to select the area for configuring Dataverse environments.

7. Build List

These questions require you to put steps in the correct order, such as deploying a Power Platform solution across environments.

Example:
Arrange these steps to deploy a solution:

1. Export from the development environment.
2. Import into the production environment.
3. Validate dependencies.

8. Lab Simulations

These questions simulate real-world tasks, such as configuring a Dataverse table, creating a Power Automate flow, or designing a Canvas app. These are hands-on scenarios that test your practical application of skills.

9. Scenario-Based Questions

These are shorter than case studies but still require you to analyze a situation and recommend solutions.

Example:
A client wants to automate customer onboarding while integrating data from multiple sources. Which Power Platform tools would you use?

10. True/False

These straightforward questions evaluate your knowledge of specific concepts, such as security, governance, or deployment strategies.

11. Inline Choice

Select the correct option(s) from drop-down menus within the question. For example, you might choose the appropriate connector for a specific integration scenario.

CHAPTER 1   GETTING STARTED WITH THE PL-600 EXAM: OVERVIEW AND ESSENTIALS

Important Features to Use

- While not a question type, this is a handy feature. If you're unsure about a question, you can mark it for review and revisit it later. Use this feature to manage your time effectively.

- A unique aspect of Microsoft exams is the "open book" feature, which allows you to access official Microsoft Learn directly within the exam tool. Here's what this means and how you can leverage it effectively during the test, but time management is very important.

8. Key Points to Remember During the Exam
Time Management

- **With Lab Simulations:** 120 minutes (2 hours).

- **Without Lab Simulations:** 100 minutes (1 hour 40 minutes).

- **Tutorial and Survey:** An additional 10–15 minutes.

- **Unscheduled Breaks:** Depending on the exam policies, you may be eligible, but certain restrictions apply, as mentioned below:

    - **No Review After a Break:** Once you take a break, you cannot review or modify the answers to questions you completed before the break.

- **Unanswered Questions Locked:** If you take a break without answering the current set of questions, those questions will be locked, and you won't be able to answer them after returning.
- **Plan Breaks Carefully:** Always complete and review the current section before taking a break to avoid losing points. By understanding these rules and planning your time wisely, you can avoid unnecessary setbacks during the exam.

Exam Room Requirements

For the PL-600 certification exam, your exam room must meet strict guidelines:

> **No Disturbances:** The space should be quiet and free from interruptions.

> **No Visitors:** No one is allowed to enter the room during the exam.

By setting up a private, distraction-free environment, you'll ensure compliance with Microsoft's policies and have a smooth testing experience.

Conclusion

So we've reached the end of Chapter 1! Let's quickly recap what we've covered:

- First off, we got a good grasp of what the PL-600 certification is all about. It's not just another Power Platform exam—it's the one that certifies your ability to design, envision, and implement solutions from end to end. If you're someone who loves connecting the dots between business needs and technology, this is your stage.

- We also touched on who this exam is for. Whether you're a functional consultant, developer, or project manager, having hands-on experience with Power Platform and Dynamics 365 gives you a solid head start. While certifications like PL-200 or PL-400 aren't mandatory, they can make your life easier when diving into the world of solution architecture.

- Then we talked about preparation. It's not just about studying hard but also studying smart. Tools like **Microsoft Learn**, practice exams, and instructor-led training are your best friends. And let's not forget—you're more likely to stay on track if you set a timeline and book that exam date early.

- We even walked through what the exam day will look like—whether you're taking it online or at a test center. Knowing the structure, question types (hello, case studies!), and how to manage your time can help calm those pre-exam nerves.

- So what's next? In the coming chapters, we're going to break down the exam's key areas, step by step, with practical insights and real-world examples. Think of this as us walking through the journey together, one concept at a time.

Remember, every step you take is progress toward not just passing the exam but truly becoming a Power Platform Solution Architect. You've got this! Let's keep the momentum going on to the next chapter!

CHAPTER 2

Building a Successful Solution Architect Framework: Key Stages and Skills

Chapter Goal: The goal of this chapter is to provide a clear overview to structure your approach as a solution architect by mastering the key stages of project execution and developing the essential skills needed for success.

Sub-topics:

1. The Path to Becoming a Solution Architect
2. Customer Discovery Essentials for a Solution Architect
3. Crafting and Proposing Effective Solutions
4. Effective Requirement Gathering: From Functional to Nonfunctional Needs
5. Assessing and Refining Requirements

CHAPTER 2   BUILDING A SUCCESSFUL SOLUTION ARCHITECT FRAMEWORK: KEY STAGES AND SKILLS

Introduction

As a solution architect, your role is pivotal in ensuring that the solutions you design not only meet the technical needs of the business but also align with its broader goals. In this chapter, we'll break down the essential steps and skills required to build a successful framework for your work as a solution architect.

The journey to becoming a proficient solution architect doesn't happen overnight. It's a combination of technical expertise, business acumen, and strong interpersonal skills. You'll need to understand how to work closely with customers, identify their unique challenges, and craft solutions that drive real value.

This chapter will guide you through key stages, starting from your path to becoming a solution architect, moving on to customer discovery, and then diving into the vital process of crafting, proposing, and refining solutions. You'll also discover how to effectively gather and assess both functional and nonfunctional requirements, ensuring that no aspect of the solution is overlooked.

By the end of this chapter, you will not only have a deeper understanding of the solution architect framework, but you'll also have practical insights that you can apply right away in your role.

The Path to Becoming a Solution Architect

A solution architect leads the design and implementation of solutions that meet both technical and business needs. They work closely with enterprise architects in larger organizations to ensure their solutions align with the broader organizational strategy.

To succeed, a solution architect needs deep knowledge of Microsoft Power Platform, Dynamics 365 apps, and related Microsoft cloud technologies. A key aspect of their role is "solution envisioning"—figuring out which parts of a problem can be solved with existing tools like Dynamics 365 and Power Platform and which require custom development through Microsoft Azure.

Solution architects act as trusted advisors, helping businesses refine their needs into effective solutions. They make decisions on development, integration, security, and more, balancing technical and business requirements. Soft skills are just as important, as they must engage effectively with business users and decision-makers. Refer to the hierarchy of solution architect in Figure 2-1.

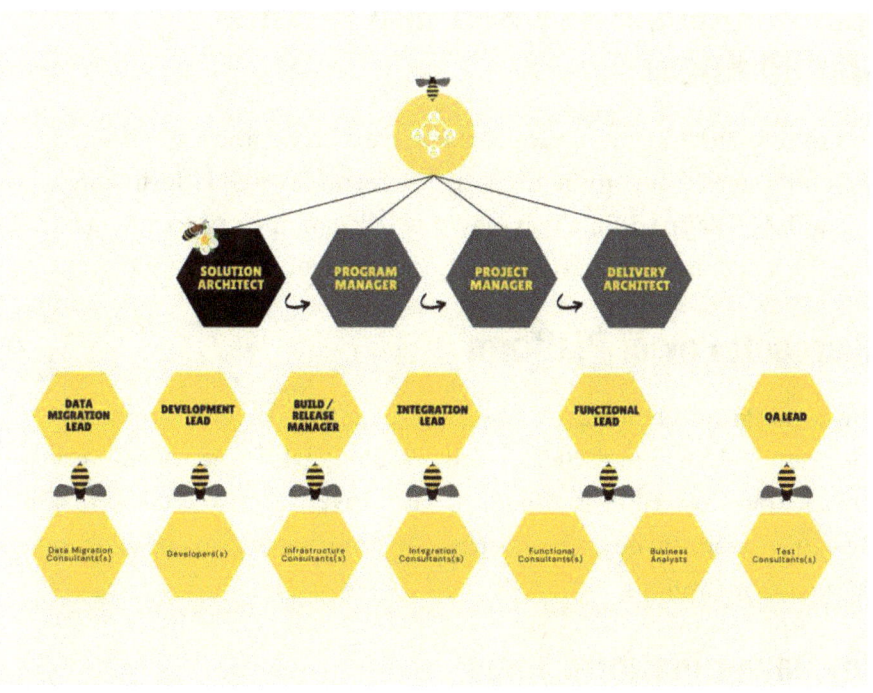

Figure 2-1. *Solution Architecture Role Organisation/Project Hierarchy*

While solution architects are often experts in certain areas, they rely on collaboration with other specialists to fill knowledge gaps. Their role spans from presales through project completion, guiding the team to deliver the best solutions.

CHAPTER 2   BUILDING A SUCCESSFUL SOLUTION ARCHITECT FRAMEWORK: KEY STAGES AND SKILLS

This module covers

- Overview of key technologies: Dynamics 365, Power Platform, and Azure
- Essential soft skills for a solution architect
- Common activities throughout the project lifecycle
- Building a solid business application architecture

Technologies Every Solution Architect Should Know

As a solution architect, it's essential to have a broad understanding of technologies that complement the Microsoft Power Platform and Dynamics 365 apps. While you may specialize in one or two, being familiar with these technologies is crucial for delivering effective solutions.

Microsoft Power Platform

Microsoft Power Platform is a powerful set of tools that helps extend Microsoft 365, Dynamics 365, and Azure, along with other third-party apps. It offers low-code automation, data-driven apps, and customizable logic to enhance business processes. Developers can also use code to extend its capabilities.

Key Power Platform Tools

- **Power BI:** Transforms data into actionable insights. Power BI connects to various data sources and helps build dashboards and reports that can be embedded into Power Apps or Power BI itself.

- **Power Apps:** Helps build apps with little to no code. There are two types: *Canvas apps*, which start with user experience design, and *Model-driven apps*, which focus on the data model.

- **Power Pages:** A low-code platform for creating external-facing business websites. Power Pages integrates seamlessly with other Power Platform tools using shared business data.

- **Power Automate:** Simplifies automation by connecting apps and services through flows. Both nontechnical users and developers can automate processes with it.

- **Data Connectors:** These let you connect Power Apps to external data sources, including SharePoint, SQL Server, and Salesforce, using prebuilt or custom connectors.

- **AI Builder:** Enables you to add AI capabilities to your apps without needing a data scientist, using pre-trained models or creating custom ones.

- **Microsoft Dataverse:** A platform to store and manage data used by business apps. It allows you to create custom entities tailored to your organization.

- **Microsoft Copilot Studio:** Helps businesses create AI-driven solutions like virtual assistants, enhancing customer and employee satisfaction.

Dynamics 365 Apps

Dynamics 365 offers a range of apps that help manage different business functions, from sales to customer service and finance. These apps integrate seamlessly with the Power Platform and Dataverse.

- **Sales, Customer Service, Field Service:** Focus on relationship management, customer satisfaction, and delivering on-site services
- **Finance, Commerce, HR, Supply Chain:** Manage finances, commerce, human resources, and supply chain operations, driving efficiency and intelligent decision-making

Other Tools and Services

- **AppSource:** A marketplace where independent software vendors (ISVs) offer solutions that may complement your Dynamics 365 or Power Platform needs.
- **Azure DevOps:** Brings together development and operations teams to improve collaboration, automate workflows, and ensure better product delivery.
- **Mixed Reality and Microsoft Copilot:** Innovations that allow blending physical and digital worlds for improved decision-making and process automation. Microsoft Copilot aids users by automating tasks and offering deeper insights through AI.

… CHAPTER 2 BUILDING A SUCCESSFUL SOLUTION ARCHITECT FRAMEWORK: KEY STAGES AND SKILLS

Key Soft Skills for a Solution Architect: 6 C's

To be successful, a solution architect needs more than just technical expertise—they must also excel in several key soft skills. These skills play a crucial role in engaging with the team and clients, and aspiring solution architects should observe how seasoned professionals handle projects to learn from their experiences. Let's learn what the 6 C's are?

1. Collaboration

While a solution architect produces key deliverables, much of the work involves collaborating with other team members. If you prefer working alone, this role might not be a great fit. A solution architect should be confident in their expertise but also open to the ideas of others. It's important to earn respect through knowledge, not authority. A good solution architect knows how to negotiate solutions with both customers and project teams.

2. Coordination

As project teams grow, coordination becomes vital. Although project managers and team lead handle much of the logistics, solution architects often have the best understanding of cross-team technical issues. For instance, coordinating between the data migration and customization teams is essential to ensure a smooth data migration. A solution architect should be skilled in driving consensus and keeping everyone on track.

3. Communication

Clear communication is key in this role. Solution architects must bridge the gap between technical and nontechnical audiences, explaining complex designs and issues in simple terms. Strong listening skills and the ability to ask clarifying questions are equally important to understand and address the real issues. Both written and verbal communication must be sharp.

4. Constructive Feedback

Providing feedback on deliverables—ranging from requirements to technical designs—is a big part of a solution architect's role. The challenge is to identify issues without making the receiver defensive. Solution architects should foster a culture of constructive feedback across teams and lead by example.

5. Crisis Management

Solution architects often tackle the toughest problems that other teams haven't been able to solve. Breaking down complex issues into manageable parts and differentiating between symptoms and causes is a crucial skill. A solution architect should approach every challenge with a problem-solving mindset, focusing on practical solutions.

6. Changeability

Finally, adaptability is what sets great solution architects apart. No two projects are the same, so being flexible and open to new challenges is essential. A positive attitude is contagious—if the solution architect stays optimistic and confident, their team will reflect that energy.

> *A solution architect's success depends not only on technical skills but also on their ability to collaborate, communicate, provide feedback, solve problems, and adapt. Leading by example and staying positive ensures that the broader project team will follow suit.*

Solution Architect Role in a Project

The role of a solution architect (SA) can vary significantly depending on the size, approach, and phase of the project. The following are common activities and responsibilities that an SA will typically engage in, often working closely with different teams across the project lifecycle.

Presales

In the presales phase, the SA supports the sales team in technical discussions to help land the project:

- **RFP Responses:** The SA handles tough technical questions that the sales team can't address, ensuring responses are feasible and aligned with the project's estimated efforts. They review others' responses to ensure accuracy and consistency.

- **Introductory Meetings:** The SA, alongside the account team, attends initial customer meetings to field technical questions and provides insights into potential solutions. This is an opportunity for the SA to understand the customer's environment, needs, and desired outcomes.

- **Proof of Concept (POC)/Demos:** The SA plays a crucial role in defining the POC or demo, helping to decide what parts of the solution to highlight. They provide deep knowledge of available prebuilt applications and integrations to ensure the demonstration is relevant.

- **Solution Envisioning:** The SA helps conceptualize a solution based on the customer's high-level needs, either during customer meetings or as an independent exercise to generate ideas. This phase can extend through the project as the solution evolves.

In presales, an essential skill for an SA is the ability to communicate effectively across different levels of the customer's organization, translating complex technical concepts into business-focused discussions. SAs also need to navigate questions clearly and avoid creating more questions than answers.

Initiation

Once the project is signed, the SA helps ensure the project is set up for success:

- **Staffing the Project Team:** The SA assists in identifying the right mix of resources for the project, ensuring that the team is equipped to meet the project's goals.
- **Defining Methodology and Processes:** The SA works with the project manager to establish the methodology, lifecycle management approach, and other essential project elements to ensure a smooth execution.

Analysis and Design

This phase involves more direct engagement from the SA as the solution begins to take shape:

- **Customer Workshops:** The SA leads workshops with business users to capture detailed requirements. The SA helps differentiate between current solutions and the real needs, ensuring the requirements are clear and implementable.

- **Requirement Validation:** The SA reviews the collected requirements, ensuring they are feasible and clear. They work with the customer to refine the requirements, adding nonfunctional needs where necessary.

- **High-Level Architecture:** The SA is responsible for defining the overall solution architecture, considering internal and external integrations and any existing systems that need to be incorporated.

- **Detailed Solution Design:** The SA takes the lead in designing detailed aspects of the solution, including security models, data structures, integration strategies, and customizations. The SA uses tools like fit-gap analysis to assess the alignment between requirements and out-of-the-box capabilities.

- **Technical Design Review:** As the team starts designing the solution in detail, the SA ensures that these designs align with the overall architecture.

Implementation

In the implementation phase, the SA ensures the solution is being built according to the defined architecture:

- **Coordination and Reviews:** The SA ensures the development teams stay aligned with the architecture. They conduct reviews to ensure the solution meets the design specifications and customer needs.

- **Problem Solving:** The SA is often called upon to resolve issues that span across multiple teams or technical domains. They leverage their holistic understanding of the project to identify solutions quickly.

- **Quality Assurance (QA):** The SA works closely with the QA team to ensure comprehensive testing, covering aspects like disaster recovery, performance, and overall system functionality.

Delivery

As the project nears completion and delivery, the SA focuses on finalizing the deployment:

- **Deployment Planning:** The SA assists in the creation of the deployment plan and validates it to ensure a smooth rollout. They may also assist in decision-making related to go/no-go during deployment.

- **Post-deployment Issues:** The SA is instrumental in triaging any issues that arise during the deployment phase, helping to quickly resolve challenges that could affect the solution's success.

Operation

Once the solution is live and in production, the SA typically has a reduced involvement, though they remain essential in the following cases:

- **Enhancements and Bugs:** If there are necessary enhancements or bugs discovered, the SA may become involved in designing the required changes.

- **Ongoing Support:** The SA is available to provide strategic guidance for ongoing improvements and to ensure the system continues to meet the business needs effectively.

CHAPTER 2   BUILDING A SUCCESSFUL SOLUTION ARCHITECT FRAMEWORK: KEY STAGES AND SKILLS

Pillars of a Great Architecture for Business Applications

The cloud has drastically transformed the way business applications are designed, allowing for more flexible, scalable, and cost-effective solutions. Solution architects today can draw from a variety of cloud services and tools to form comprehensive solutions. These include

- Dynamics 365
- Microsoft 365
- AppSource
- Extending with Microsoft Power Platform
- Microsoft Azure
- Microsoft Copilot

Though there is no single blueprint for designing a perfect architecture, there are several key principles that can guide solution architects in creating business application solutions that meet both technical and business needs.

1. Security

Security is paramount for any application, especially in a cloud environment where sensitive data is often accessed over networks. As data is one of an organization's most valuable assets, securing it from unauthorized access or threats is crucial.

Key Considerations

- **Authentication and Access Control:** Implement strong authentication mechanisms to secure access to your architecture.

- **Encryption and Data Protection:** Use encryption for sensitive data, both at rest and in transit.

- **Security Features:** Utilize Azure Conditional Access, Data Loss Prevention (DLP) policies, and secure key management practices (secrets, certificates).

- **Lifecycle Security:** Ensure security practices are embedded in the application's lifecycle—from design to operation.

By securing both the perimeter and data access layers, a solution architect ensures that only authorized users can access sensitive data without overwhelming the system's maintainability.

2. Empowering End Users

A great solution architecture fosters empowerment for users, allowing them to create tools or extensions they need without compromising the integrity of the solution.

Key Considerations

- **Low-Code/No-Code Solutions:** Use tools like Microsoft Power Platform to enable nontechnical users to develop applications that enhance productivity.

- **Templates and Starter Apps:** Provide pre-configured templates, reusable Power Apps components, and connectors to help users quickly create their own tools.

- **Guardrails and Governance:** Ensure that self-service solutions are built within secure boundaries, fostering innovation while maintaining control over the environment.

- **Center of Excellence:** Establish a center of excellence with best practices, training, and governance to guide user innovation.

By fostering a culture of innovation, you empower users to meet their needs independently, while the architecture provides oversight to prevent chaos.

3. Trust and Privacy

Compliance and privacy are critical for organizations operating in regulated industries or regions with strict data privacy laws.

Key Considerations

- **Compliance Frameworks:** Familiarize yourself with Microsoft's Trust Center, which offers tools and certifications to help ensure solutions meet regulatory requirements.

- **Data Privacy:** Ensure that data handling practices align with industry-specific regulations (e.g., GDPR, HIPAA).

- **Privacy Requests:** Implement the necessary mechanisms to respond to privacy regulation requests, ensuring your customers' data rights are protected.

A solution that adheres to trust and privacy regulations builds customer confidence and meets legal obligations.

4. Maintainability

A successful architecture should be designed with future maintenance in mind. Solutions should avoid excessive custom code, as this can create technical debt, making future updates more complex and costly.

Key Considerations

- **Customization vs. Configuration:** Prefer using the platform's configuration and customization tools over custom code, ensuring easier maintenance and future updates.

- **Documentation:** Maintain thorough documentation and comments for the technical implementation, enabling future developers or administrators to understand the system.

- **Minimize Technical Debt:** Design with scalability and long-term support in mind, reducing the need for frequent adjustments.

Maintainability ensures that the solution can adapt and evolve with minimal cost and effort over time.

5. Availability and Recoverability

One of the key principles in cloud-based solution architecture is anticipating and mitigating failures. An architect's job is to design a solution that ensures uptime and allows for quick recovery if issues arise.

Key Considerations

- **Failover and Redundancy:** Design the solution with high availability in mind, using redundant systems and failover mechanisms to minimize downtime.

- **Recovery Plans:** Ensure that recovery time objectives (RTOs) and recovery point objectives (RPOs) are met.

- **Testing:** Regularly test the backup and recovery processes to ensure they are effective during failures.

Architecting for availability and recoverability ensures that the system can continue to serve users even in the face of potential disruptions.

6. Performance and Scalability

For cloud-based solutions to be effective, they must meet user demands while scaling to handle increased load over time.

Key Considerations

- **Dynamic Scaling:** Use cloud capabilities to automatically scale resources based on demand, ensuring efficient use of resources.

- **Performance Metrics:** Identify and monitor key performance indicators (KPIs) like response time, transaction throughput, and system resource utilization.

- **Load Balancing:** Implement load-balancing techniques to distribute workloads efficiently across servers or cloud resources.

By matching resource capacity to demand, you ensure that the solution performs optimally under various usage conditions.

7. Efficiency and Operations

Cost-effective operations are a critical component of cloud architecture. Efficiency in cloud environments helps reduce waste and maximize resource utilization.

Key Considerations

- **Cost Monitoring:** Use cloud monitoring tools to track and analyze resource usage, identifying areas where costs can be reduced.

- **Automation:** Implement automation for routine tasks to reduce operational overhead.

- **Monitoring and Alerts:** Set up robust monitoring systems that provide real-time data and alerts, enabling teams to detect and respond to issues before they impact users.

Efficient operations ensure that the solution remains cost-effective while delivering maximum value to the business.

8. Shared Responsibility

In the cloud, the responsibility for managing infrastructure is shared between the provider (e.g., Microsoft Azure) and the customer (the solution architect). Understanding this division of responsibility is crucial for making sound architectural decisions.

Key Considerations

- **Cloud Provider's Role:** The cloud provider manages aspects like the physical infrastructure, network security, and platform services.

- **Customer's Role:** The customer is responsible for managing the application, its data, user access, and configuration.

- **Impact on Design:** Architects need to consider how this shared responsibility model affects operational capabilities, cost, and security decisions.

The shared responsibility model shifts non-core activities to the cloud provider, freeing up architects to focus on delivering business value.

9. Design Choices and Trade-offs

In designing a solution, an architect must make decisions that balance multiple pillars (e.g., security, performance, cost) based on the organization's priorities and constraints.

Key Considerations

- **Trade-offs:** Building a solution that is both secure, high-performing, and cost-effective often requires trade-offs. Architects need to evaluate the relative importance of each pillar and adjust design decisions accordingly.

- **Cost vs. Performance:** Higher performance often comes with increased costs, so architects must decide the acceptable trade-offs based on business goals.

- **Risk Management:** Consider the potential risks associated with each design choice, particularly in areas like security, scalability, and compliance.

Every design decision involves balancing priorities, ensuring that the final solution aligns with the organization's objectives.

Summary

Becoming a solution architect requires a combination of technical expertise and strong soft skills. The architect must be proficient in technologies such as Dynamics 365, Microsoft 365, Power Platform, and Azure, as these are the core tools used to build effective business solutions. In addition to technical proficiency, soft skills like the 6 C's - Colloboration, Co-Ordination, Communication, Constructive Feedback, Crisis Management, Changeability—are essential for successful interactions with customers and teams. These skills help architects navigate complex project challenges, communicate effectively, and adapt to changing requirements. The solution architect's role spans from presales, where they support the sales team and engage with customers, to post-implementation, ensuring the solution aligns with business needs. Key responsibilities include leading workshops, defining high-level architecture, ensuring security and compliance, and promoting scalability and performance. Pillars of a great architecture for business applications involve considerations like security, maintainability, availability, performance, and cost efficiency. By balancing these pillars, solution architects deliver robust and sustainable business applications that meet organizational goals.

CHAPTER 2   BUILDING A SUCCESSFUL SOLUTION ARCHITECT FRAMEWORK: KEY STAGES AND SKILLS

Customer Discovery Essentials for a Solution Architect

Introduction

Customer discovery is a key phase in any solution architecture process. It helps a solution architect understand the true needs of the customer and design a system that effectively meets those needs. This process doesn't end after the first meeting or even the first project; it is an ongoing engagement with the customer to adapt and refine the solution based on evolving requirements.

At the heart of customer discovery is the critical question, "Why?" Understanding the "why" behind each request or concern allows the architect to dig deeper into the customer's goals and motivations, uncovering their true needs. However, the "Why?" question may need to be adjusted depending on the context to gain a comprehensive understanding of the situation.

For instance, if a customer requests a feature such as adding a button to a screen, a solution architect should probe further with a question like "What is the outcome you're expecting once the task on this screen is completed?" This shift in perspective allows for identifying the underlying need rather than focusing only on the technical request.

Key Topics Covered in Customer Discovery

1. **Initial Customer Discovery**

    This phase begins before the customer even becomes a client. It involves researching their operations, industry, and any public details that could inform the engagement. You must prepare by understanding their structure, business model, and pain points, as well as learning about any existing solutions they might have in place.

2. **Managing Customer Discovery Meetings**

    Discovery meetings are essential to gather information. Preparing for these meetings is critical. It's important to develop a structured agenda, set objectives, and establish a plan for follow-up. This way, you can make the most of the limited time you have with the customer.

3. **Learning Through Interviews and Interactions**

    Listening to interviews, especially between experienced solution architects and customers, can provide useful insights into how communication should be handled and how solutions can be aligned with customer expectations.

4. **Evaluating Customer Needs Beyond a Checklist**

    While gathering requirements is often seen as simply ticking off items on a list, the real challenge lies in interpreting those needs. The goal is to understand the customer's goals and how the solution can add value, rather than merely fulfilling technical requirements.

CHAPTER 2   BUILDING A SUCCESSFUL SOLUTION ARCHITECT FRAMEWORK: KEY STAGES AND SKILLS

Initial Customer Discovery: The Process

Learning About Your Customer

Customer discovery begins with gathering public data. Information from various sources, such as the company's website, social media profiles, and news articles, can provide useful background. For example, the company's website often includes details about their vision, offerings, and the departments or lines of business relevant to your engagement. This knowledge helps create a stronger connection and understanding of the customer's business operations.

Important Resources to Leverage

1. **Company Website:** Start by reviewing the company's history, mission statement, and goals. This can offer insights into their strategic direction and areas where they may need support.

2. **Social Media:** Use platforms like LinkedIn to understand more about key decision-makers, company culture, and recent achievements or challenges.

3. **Public News Outlets:** Gain insight into the company's market reputation, financial health, and any major changes like mergers, acquisitions, or product launches.

4. **Request for Proposal (RFP):** Often, the RFP outlines a formal set of requirements, which can serve as a foundation for understanding what the customer is looking for.

Developing Probing Questions: Once you have a general understanding of the customer's operations, you can begin to craft probing questions that will help refine the solution. Probing questions are designed to extract further details that may not be immediately obvious, helping you better align the solution with the customer's objectives.

Sample Questions for LK Tech Solutions

1. **Public Perception of LK Tech Solutions**

   "What is the public perception of **LK Tech** in the EdTech industry? Why is it important to improve or maintain this perception?"

   - *Objective:* Understand the company's brand value and how it aligns with their strategic goals.

2. **Stakeholder Roles and Motivation**

   "What are the backgrounds and roles of the project owners, stakeholders, and decision-makers? Why were they chosen for this project?"

   - *Objective:* Gauge the decision-makers' level of expertise and how they prioritize certain goals over others.

3. **Legacy Data and Systems**

   "Does LK Tech have legacy data or systems that need to be migrated to the new solution? Why is this data critical to the project?"

   - *Objective:* Understand any dependencies on legacy systems and the potential challenges of migrating data.

4. **Data Location and Security**

   "What are LK Tech's concerns about the location and security of data? Why are these concerns significant for your operations?"

   - *Objective:* Ensure the solution complies with regulatory and security standards.

5. **Measuring Training Program Success**

   "How does LK Tech currently measure the success of its training programs, and why do these metrics matter for the new system?"

   - *Objective:* Identify KPIs and ensure that the new system will provide the necessary functionality to track those KPIs effectively.

Discovery Meetings

Discovery meetings can take various forms, depending on the stage of the engagement. Below are a few common meeting types:

1. **Workshops**

   Workshops are highly interactive and allow stakeholders to collaborate and provide insights. These sessions often include brainstorming, role-playing, and wireframing activities.

2. **Surveys**

   Targeted surveys can help gather information from a larger pool of stakeholders. Surveys are especially useful for collecting anonymous feedback from users who may not feel comfortable speaking up in meetings.

CHAPTER 2   BUILDING A SUCCESSFUL SOLUTION ARCHITECT FRAMEWORK: KEY STAGES AND SKILLS

3. **Job Shadowing**

    This involves following a user through their daily tasks to understand the pain points they face in their workflow. Observing users in action can reveal inefficiencies that may not be immediately apparent.

Customer Communication Strategy for Solution Architects

A clear and effective customer communication strategy is vital in the discovery process to ensure alignment and build trust with the customer. The strategy includes various components, methods, and tools to facilitate continuous and transparent communication throughout the solution design phase. Here's an outline of a communication strategy for solution architects during the customer discovery phase.

Initial Contact and Relationship Building

- **Objective:** Establish trust and begin building a partnership with the customer.

- **Approach:** Use an introductory meeting to understand the customer's business, mission, and challenges. Focus on rapport-building and create a welcoming environment to encourage open communication.

- **Tools/Methods:** Email, video conferencing, and face-to-face meetings.

Active Listening and Empathy

- **Objective:** Truly understand the customer's pain points, goals, and aspirations.

- **Approach:** Engage in active listening during all discovery sessions, making sure to ask open-ended questions, reflect on responses, and dig deeper into the customer's underlying needs.

- **Tools/Methods:** One-on-one interviews, collaborative workshops, and needs assessment surveys.

Frequent Updates and Transparency

- **Objective:** Keep the customer informed on the progress of the discovery phase and ensure their concerns are addressed in real time.

- **Approach:** Provide regular updates to the customer on findings, challenges, and next steps. Address any potential misunderstandings or misalignments immediately.

- **Tools/Methods:** Weekly reports, progress meetings, project management tools like Microsoft Teams or Asana, and email summaries.

Tailored Communication for Different Stakeholders

- **Objective:** Communicate effectively with various customer stakeholders, each having different needs and priorities.

- **Approach:** Customize communication based on the stakeholder's role and decision-making authority. For example, technical teams may need in-depth technical details, while executives may require a high-level overview of business impact.

- **Tools/Methods:** Stakeholder mapping, personalized email communication, executive briefings, and technical workshops.

Clarification of Requirements and Expectations

- **Objective:** Ensure there is no ambiguity in customer requirements and expectations.

- **Approach:** Regularly validate the customer's expectations, assumptions, and requirements through documentation, confirmation meetings, and feedback loops. Use visual aids and prototypes to clarify complex concepts.

- **Tools/Methods:** Use project charters, solution diagrams, and interactive prototypes for better clarity.

Continuous Engagement and Collaboration

- **Objective:** Engage the customer throughout the process, ensuring they feel involved and heard.

- **Approach:** Involve the customer in decision-making, such as prioritizing requirements and reviewing prototypes. Encourage feedback loops and ensure that the customer's input shapes the solution being proposed.

- **Tools/Methods:** Collaborative tools like Microsoft SharePoint, Teams, or a shared document repository for real-time co-authoring.

Feedback and Iteration

- **Objective:** Refine the solution based on continuous customer feedback.

- **Approach:** After each interaction or milestone, request customer feedback on the proposed solutions or requirements. Use this feedback to iterate and improve the design before moving to the next stage.

- **Tools/Methods:** Surveys, feedback forms, and retrospective meetings.

Defining Success and Aligning on Outcomes

- **Objective:** Ensure the customer understands and agrees on what success looks like.

- **Approach:** Collaboratively define clear success metrics with the customer that will help both parties evaluate the effectiveness of the solution.

- **Tools/Methods:** Success criteria templates, KPI discussions, and post-engagement surveys.

Building Long-Term Relationships

- **Objective:** Maintain a relationship with the customer even after the solution is delivered.

- **Approach:** Continue to provide value by offering support, post-implementation reviews, and identifying opportunities for future collaboration.

- **Tools/Methods:** Regular follow-up meetings, customer satisfaction surveys, and quarterly business reviews.

By implementing a thoughtful and structured communication strategy, solution architects can ensure that their customers' needs are thoroughly understood and addressed, paving the way for successful project outcomes and long-lasting partnerships.

Summary

Customer discovery is a fundamental process for solution architects, focusing on understanding a customer's true needs to design the most effective solutions. It involves asking the right questions and going beyond surface-level requirements to uncover the underlying motivations behind customer requests. The process includes initial research into the customer's business, ongoing interactions, and using targeted questions to explore key pain points and goals.

The unit outlines how to manage discovery meetings, learn about customers through interviews, and evaluate needs beyond checklists. It emphasizes the importance of understanding the customer's operations, industry, and existing systems to create tailored solutions. A key component of discovery is the development of probing questions, which help clarify the customer's real objectives.

CHAPTER 2   BUILDING A SUCCESSFUL SOLUTION ARCHITECT FRAMEWORK: KEY STAGES AND SKILLS

Using the example of **LK Tech Solutions**, an EdTech company with operational inefficiencies, the chapter explores how to gather information, evaluate stakeholders, and define success criteria. It also highlights various discovery meeting types like workshops, surveys, and job shadowing, each providing a different method for gathering insights.

Ultimately, customer discovery is about continuously aligning the solution with the customer's evolving needs and defining success through measurable outcomes.

Crafting and Proposing Effective Solutions

Introduction

This is designed to guide learners in effectively identifying, crafting, and presenting solutions tailored to meet the needs of a business. It focuses on how to assess a problem, develop a solution, and propose that solution to stakeholders, making it a vital resource for individuals looking to develop skills in solution-oriented thinking and problem-solving. The module is particularly beneficial for those in roles such as solution architects, business analysts, and consultants who are responsible for recommending and implementing business technology solutions.

A Structured Approach for Solution Architects

Proposing a solution is a crucial phase in the project lifecycle, where the solution architect starts to translate the customer's needs and business requirements into tangible solutions. At this point, the details may not be sufficient for long-term planning, but it's an opportunity to create a proof of concept (PoC) to demonstrate the solution's feasibility.

Here's a refined and structured approach for crafting and proposing effective solutions:

CHAPTER 2   BUILDING A SUCCESSFUL SOLUTION ARCHITECT FRAMEWORK: KEY STAGES AND SKILLS

1. Solution Design and Proof of Concept

- **Objective:** Translate customer needs into a feasible solution while considering existing systems and constraints.

- **Considerations**

  - Evaluate the current systems and applications in place to understand what can be leveraged and what must remain unchanged.

  - Identify any constraints, such as legacy systems or regulations that must be accounted for during the solution design process.

  - Develop a proof of concept (PoC) or prototype applications that allow the customer to visualize how the proposed solution can meet their needs.

- **Tools/Methods:** Use mock-ups, wireframes, or simple prototypes to illustrate key features of the solution, demonstrating how it aligns with the customer's expectations.

2. Customization vs. Extension

- **Objective:** Strike a balance between customizing the solution and leveraging out-of-the-box functionalities to avoid excessive technical debt.

- **Key Considerations**

  - **Customization:** Tailoring the solution with custom code or specific features to meet the customer's unique needs. However, excessive customizations can increase costs and create future maintenance challenges (technical debt).

- **Extension:** Extending existing functionalities, such as adding new features or integrating with other systems, rather than completely customizing them.

- **Transparent Decision-Making:** Ensure that the customer understands the long-term cost implications of customizations and the benefits of leveraging standard features.

• **Rule Setting:** Implement guidelines to manage the decision-making process for customizations. For instance, if a feature requires more than two days to configure or necessitates writing custom code, it should be approved by senior leadership (e.g., CTO). This ensures cost-effective decision-making while maintaining transparency.

• **Customer Engagement:** Explain the rationale behind proposed solutions and offer simpler, out-of-the-box alternatives when possible. This approach often results in greater customer satisfaction.

3. Documenting Requirements Early

- **Objective:** Create a clear and thorough record of the customer's requirements from the beginning to guide the solution development process.

- **Key Document: Solution Blueprint**
    - Like a construction blueprint, a solution blueprint serves as the architectural plan for the solution.
    - It outlines the key components of the solution, such as

- **Process Architecture:** How business processes will be mapped and automated
- **Application Architecture:** How various applications will interact and integrate
- **Data Architecture:** Data models, storage solutions, and data flow
- **Integration Architecture:** Integration with existing systems or third-party applications
- **Intelligence Architecture:** Use of AI, machine learning, or analytics within the solution
- **Security Architecture:** Security protocols, user authentication, and access control
- **Continuous Update:** How the solution will receive updates or enhancements post-deployment
- **Platform Architecture:** Overview of the platform hosting the solution (e.g., Microsoft Azure, on-premises)

- **Tools/Methods:** Create diagrams, charts, and other visual representations to illustrate how the solution will operate. This helps align technical and business teams, providing a clear path forward.

4. Identifying Solution Components

- **Objective:** Break down the solution into core components that are necessary for delivering the solution.

- **Key Steps**
  - Identify the **primary building blocks** of the solution (e.g., software, hardware, services, and third-party applications).
  - Ensure each component contributes to meeting the business and technical requirements defined during the discovery phase.
- **Tools/Methods:** Use flowcharts, mind maps, and architecture modeling tools to identify and organize solution components.

5. Developing and Validating Proof of Concept (PoC)

- **Objective:** Develop a PoC to validate the feasibility of the solution and its alignment with customer needs.
- **Key Considerations**
  - Ensure the PoC covers key functionalities that will be critical to the final solution.
  - Engage the customer throughout the PoC phase to gather feedback and ensure alignment.
  - Validate whether the solution meets technical requirements, scalability, and performance expectations.
- **Tools/Methods:** Rapid prototyping tools, Power Apps, and demo environments.

6. Identifying Potential Third-Party Components

- **Objective:** Identify and evaluate third-party tools, software, or services that can complement the solution.

- **Key Considerations**
  - Ensure that third-party components integrate seamlessly with the solution and align with the customer's needs.
  - Evaluate the pros and cons of using third-party tools, considering factors such as cost, compatibility, and vendor support.

- **Tools/Methods:** Market research, third-party vendor assessments, and integration testing.

7. Recognizing Strengths and Weaknesses in the Solution

- **Objective:** Analyze the proposed solution's strengths and weaknesses to ensure it delivers the best value to the customer.

- **Key Steps**
  - Perform a **SWOT analysis** (Strengths, Weaknesses, Opportunities, Threats) for the solution to identify potential challenges and areas for improvement.
  - Engage the customer in this process by seeking their feedback on perceived strengths and risks.
  - Propose mitigation strategies for any identified weaknesses or risks, such as offering additional support, training, or solution enhancements.

Identifying and Proposing Solution Components: A Presales Approach

As you move forward in the discovery and presales phase, you'll begin to define the key components of your proposed solution. At this stage, your goal is not to deliver a full-fledged solution but to illustrate a clear picture for the customer of how their objectives will be met, emphasizing the value and potential outcomes of the proposed solution. Here's a structured approach to identifying and organizing solution components.

1. Mapping Customer Needs to Functionality

During discovery, you've gathered vital insights into your customer's key business needs. The next step is to map these needs to available components. This may involve

- **Dynamics 365 Apps:** Existing applications that can fulfill some or all of the customer's requirements.

- **Custom Microsoft Power Platform Apps:** Where Dynamics 365 apps fall short, Power Platform solutions may fill the gap, such as Power Apps, Power Automate, or Power BI.

- **Custom Development:** In some cases, requirements will need custom development, either through the Power Platform or other technologies.

Many projects are enhancements or integrations with existing systems, and you need to consider how to leverage what the customer already has in place, for example, integrating Dynamics 365 Customer Service with new omnichannel features.

2. Customization vs. Out-of-the-Box Solutions

Customization can add significant cost and complexity. While it might seem easier to tailor a solution with heavy customization, it often leads to technical debt. It's crucial to set expectations up front regarding the real cost of customizations. Highlight when you are using out-of-the-box functionality and where customization is necessary.

For example, a product configurator might require custom development, but other aspects of the sales process might use out-of-the-box Dynamics 365 features. You can create internal rules that define when customization is justified, such as if the feature takes more than two days to configure or requires additional code.

3. Solution Blueprint Documentation

A solution blueprint is crucial for aligning everyone on the architecture and components of the solution. While a full blueprint comes later, during the presales phase, you can start drafting this document based on the information collected in the discovery process. A blueprint includes several types of architecture, which may include

- **Process Architecture:** Defining key business processes and how they will be supported
- **Application Architecture:** Mapping out the systems and applications involved
- **Data Architecture:** Defining the flow of data, storage, and access control
- **Integration Architecture:** Identifying how the solution integrates with existing systems
- **Security Architecture:** Ensuring data protection, access control, and compliance

- **Continuous Update Architecture:** Managing ongoing changes and system updates

- **Platform Architecture:** Ensuring scalability and compatibility with the platform

- **Deployment Architecture:** Ensuring faster deployment to any environments with validation

4. User Experience and Wireframes

In the discovery phase, it's essential to understand how the solution will be used by different user types, especially mobile or remote users. User experience is often the focal point for customers, and you need to capture any specific needs here. A wireframe or mock-up can help demonstrate how the solution will meet these needs.

5. Process and Data Modeling

Process Modeling: Once you've identified the key processes, you should explain how the solution will improve or transform them. This could mean automating steps or reducing bottlenecks, and you should emphasize the benefits these changes will bring.

  Data Modeling: While formal data modeling happens later in the design phase, high-level conceptualization can begin during presales. You can create summary data models to explain the flow and structure of the key data involved.

6. Identifying Third-Party Components

Sometimes, your solution will involve third-party components. This is where identifying dependencies on third-party vendors or systems becomes crucial. Ensure that you clearly define how these components will be integrated into your solution, specifying who is responsible for their management and how they will interact with the rest of the solution and ensure third-party component security and vulnerability test.

7. Integration with Existing Systems

A large portion of most solutions will involve integrations with other internal or external systems. Clear definition of the boundaries where one system ends and another begins is vital to ensure smooth integration. Establishing clear contracts on who builds and manages the integration points helps avoid confusion and responsibility gaps.

8. Deployment Options

Microsoft offers various deployment models for Dynamics 365, which can be deployed in the cloud or on-premises. Depending on the application, the deployment might require Lifecycle Services (LCS) or standard cloud environments. Additionally, defining whether you will use trial, sandbox, or production environments early on is important for the presales phase.

9. Next Steps and Solution Refinement

The goal at this stage is not to design the entire solution but to outline a clear vision of how the customer's needs will be met. Identify the next steps, which might include

- Finalizing a demo or proof of concept
- Tailoring a solution to the customer's specific requirements
- Moving forward with pricing and contract finalization

By identifying solution components and creating early documentation, you'll be well-prepared for the next stages of your project, ensuring a smooth transition from presales to implementation.

Develop and Validate a Demo

As you start to envision the solution that you will propose, you might consider sharing a demo to validate requirements with your stakeholders and to help build confidence in the platform. When a customer is confident in the platform, they are more willing to accept your proposed solutions with enthusiasm.

Demos can take different shapes and forms, depending on the solution that is being proposed. The following approaches are some of the most common:

- **Out-of-the-Box:** This type of demonstration highlights one or more of the apps that don't have customizations. This demo is often performed by presales resources and doesn't involve the solution architect. This method is an effective way to get customers up to date with the core product features. The negative aspect of this approach is that it doesn't help the customer envision their solution on the app. You can mitigate this issue by including relevant sample data to their business.

- **Prebuilt Demo:** Many partners specialize in particular verticals or solution areas and invest in developing prebuilt demos that contain their own intellectual property that tailors the out-of-the-box base solution with their designed Value-added Designs. This approach helps the customer see their problem area because it often uses the vertical language in the app.

Additionally, this type of demo hides topics that aren't appropriate for the solution area that might distract the customer. While the solution architect isn't typically involved in demonstrating this prebuilt solution, they were likely involved in helping compose it at some point. In fact, the solution architect should potentially consider proposing demonstrating the prebuilt solution when they find themselves building the same prototypes repeatedly.

- **Prototype:** This approach takes the out-of-the-box state and, with the customer's needs in mind, performs minimal tailoring of the app to reflect the customer's needs. The main benefit of this method is to help the solution architect to tell a story during the demo that the customer can relate to when trying to solve their particular objectives. The solution architect is often involved in helping customers identify their objectives by using the envisioned solution to help either build or guide the team to produce the prototype.

- **Proof of Concept:** Proofs of concept should be built to prove that a concept works and typically involves a specific component or activity in the proposed solution. Frequently, this method is done during the design phase but can also be used during presales when the customer needs to see the concept work in the context of their proposed solution. The solution architect typically drives the need for this method and is involved in driving the effort. Unlike a prototype that usually has a straightforward path to completion, proofs of concept might try multiple approaches to reach the desired goal.

It's common to interchangeably use the prototype and proof-of-concept approaches, and from a customer's perspective, the difference typically doesn't matter. Your goal should be focused on telling a story and bringing your proposed solution to life, which will help the customer see their problem solved by the proposed solution. You should also consider reducing risk by eliminating unknown issues that might contribute to the customer's current problem.

Solution Architect Involvement

The solution architect, along with the sales team, should be involved in identifying what should be demoed and what approach to use (e.g., out-of-the-box vs. prototype).

How involved a solution architect should be in building a prototype or proof of concept varies greatly across projects. These efforts commonly involve multiple skill sets and a decision point of who should be involved in building. Often, the solution architect will find that if they simply do all the work themselves, it might take a few hours, whereas coordinating across a team of diverse resources and having to explain the need might take a few weeks. Solution architects should make sure that they involve others in situations where it's not advantageous to complete the work by themselves.

Keep or Discard

When you build a prototype or proof of concept, you should realize that quick wins might not translate to a best practice for production-ready solutions. Best practices aren't difficult to follow; however, if you want to quickly showcase an idea, it's easier to develop an impromptu idea than use an established best practice to plan for a larger solution. You should decide on this approach in advance because if you want to carry the assets forward, you will need to ensure that these assets meet your standards and aren't shortcuts that can't be remedied easily.

Manage Expectations

Creating a demo to showcase your proposed solution can be almost effortless; therefore, it is important to manage your expectations. Commonly, after a demo has been given, a customer immediately accepts the proposal and asks when they can go live with the solution. The best way to manage this scenario is to be direct by saying that while what you are showing might look complete, it doesn't have all the security, automation, and other enhancements that are necessary for going live. It's important to have this discussion right away rather than assuming that the customer understands that your demo is simply a demonstration and not the final solution.

Identifying Potential Third-Party Components for Your Solution

During a project, you might face situations where the app you're working with can't meet certain requirements. At this point, you have three options:

1. Custom-build a new app
2. Look for a third-party solution
3. Work with the customer to modify the requirements

However, the best approach is usually to prioritize out-of-the-box solutions. This minimizes complexity and helps keep licensing and maintenance costs manageable. But if third-party components are necessary, here's how you can go about selecting them wisely.

Where to Find Third-Party Solutions

One of the best places to look for third-party solutions is **AppSource**, Microsoft's official app marketplace. Independent software vendors (ISVs) can list their solutions here after going through a certification process.

When evaluating third-party solutions, it's crucial to consider the level of integration with Microsoft Power Platform or Dynamics 365 apps you're using. If a solution isn't fully integrated, you might need to invest in custom integrations, which could add complexity and cost.

Solution architects in the same domain often keep track of the most popular ISVs and their solutions. Many partners develop expertise in certain ISV extensions, which they can reuse in future engagements. This internal evaluation and selection process is usually led by the solution architect.

Evaluating the ISV (Independent Software Vendor)

When you decide to include an ISV component, you're depending on the long-term viability of that component and its vendor. The future success of your project depends on the ISV's ability to deliver as promised. Here are some key factors to consider when evaluating an ISV:

- **How long has the ISV been in business?**

    A well-established ISV is more likely to be reliable and sustainable.

- **How large is the ISV, and do they have the resources to support your project?**

    Make sure the ISV has the capabilities to handle implementations of your size.

- **How long have they been building solutions for Microsoft Power Platform or Dynamics 365?**

  An ISV with extensive experience in Microsoft technologies is more likely to understand the ecosystem and its requirements.

Evaluating the ISV Component

Before committing to a third-party solution, you should assess whether the ISV component can adequately address the specific problem you're solving. Here are some critical factors to evaluate:

- **Security Integration**

  Does the component integrate smoothly with Microsoft Power Platform and/or Dynamics 365 security models? If not, how easy is it to align the two models while meeting security requirements?

- **Flexibility for Customization**

  Consider the customization options offered by the component. Does it allow enough flexibility to meet your business needs, or will you be forced to adapt your requirements to fit its limitations?

- **Keeping Up with Microsoft Releases**

  Microsoft releases updates regularly, so it's important to check if the ISV stays current with these updates. The component should follow best practices and supported techniques to ensure compatibility with the latest Microsoft releases.

- **ISV Roadmap**

    Check the ISV's roadmap to understand their plans for future enhancements. It's vital to know if the product will continue evolving or if it's essentially an "as-is" offering.

- **Data Location**

    Understand where the ISV stores its data. Does it integrate well with your Microsoft Power Platform and/or Dynamics 365 apps? Alternatively, does it use its own storage solution? You need to ensure compliance with data governance requirements.

- **Fitting the Gap**

    If your team plans to further customize the component, verify that its licensing allows for such customizations. Additionally, assess any potential technical debt that might arise from these customizations.

Evaluating Licensing

Licensing is a crucial factor when incorporating a third-party component. Ensure that the cost of licensing is not only covered in the project budget but that it's also compatible with your intended usage. For example, check if the third-party solution has limits on API calls or other usage metrics that might not align with your project's volume.

While **open source** solutions are becoming more popular due to their cost-effectiveness, you should still carefully evaluate the licensing model and any compliance requirements. Some contracts with customers may stipulate approval for open source components before they can be included in the solution.

CHAPTER 2   BUILDING A SUCCESSFUL SOLUTION ARCHITECT FRAMEWORK: KEY STAGES AND SKILLS

Recognizing Strengths and Weaknesses in a Solution

As a solution architect, one of the critical challenges you face is becoming too close to the solution you have proposed or designed. It's easy to lose perspective on the strengths and weaknesses of the solution during the design and implementation phases. Regular reflection and periodic assessments are essential to ensure that your solution meets the objectives and provides value to the customer. This chapter explores how to evaluate the solution and address key areas like organizational objectives, over-solving, competition, and potential weaknesses.

1. Addressing Organizational Objectives

When developing a solution, always keep the customer's organizational objectives at the forefront. These objectives should guide the design and help determine whether the solution is adequately addressing the customer's needs.

Key Considerations

- **Review Your Objectives:** Ensure that the objectives are clear, concise, and actionable. Having objectives that are too broad or ambiguous can lead to confusion or misalignment during the project's execution.

- **Reflect on Completeness:** Evaluate if more information can be added to further demonstrate how the solution will meet customer goals. Sometimes, an alternative solution might provide even better value.

- **Collaboration:** Work with other architects or stakeholders who may have a fresh perspective. An external viewpoint can identify whether certain aspects of your solution are unnecessary or if you've overlooked potential value additions.

2. Over-solving a Problem

Sometimes architects, especially those who are experienced with certain tools or technologies, can be inclined to propose complex solutions. While the intent is to cover all aspects of the problem, this can lead to over-engineering, adding unnecessary complexity.

Key Considerations

- **Avoid Proposing Overly Complex Solutions:** Before finalizing your design, ask yourself whether the proposed app or solution is disproportionate to the customer's actual needs. Does the solution require excessive customization? Could a simpler approach achieve the same outcomes?

- **Scope Creep:** Keep the solution focused on addressing the problem at hand. Over-solving can lead to scope creep, which complicates implementation and escalates costs without providing significant value.

3. Customizing an App vs. Using a Prebuilt App

When custom-built solutions are proposed, there may be opportunities to leverage prebuilt apps or existing components. Microsoft's **Dynamics 365** or the **AppSource** marketplace offers a wide range of solutions that can often meet customer requirements with less effort than building a custom solution.

Key Considerations

- **Prebuilt vs. Custom-Built:** Evaluate whether certain parts of the solution can be fulfilled by an existing app or component. This approach is often more cost-effective, scalable, and time-efficient than building custom components from scratch.

- **Discuss Options with the Customer:** Especially during the presales phase, offer a range of options for the customer to choose from. This creates an opportunity to discuss the pros and cons of each option, including licensing, maintenance, and scalability.

4. Compare Your Proposed Solution with the Competition

In a competitive landscape, it is likely that your proposal is being evaluated alongside other solutions from different vendors, including those based on Microsoft technologies or even other competitive vendors.

Key Considerations

- **Understand Your Competition:** Take time to research and understand other solutions being presented to the customer. Knowing the strengths and weaknesses of competitor solutions will allow you to defend your proposal more effectively.

- **Prepare Your Sales Team:** Equip your sales team with a comprehensive understanding of your solution's benefits, unique selling points (USPs), and how it compares to competitors. Having this information readily available can be crucial when discussions about different solutions arise.

5. Identifying Organizational Opportunities

During the discovery phase, the customer may have shared a variety of challenges beyond the current scope. These additional challenges can present valuable opportunities for improvement.

Key Considerations

- **Review Uncovered Challenges:** As you finalize the proposed solution, revisit the other challenges the customer faced. If some of these are closely related to your solution, consider adding them to the scope of your proposal.

- **Easy Wins:** Often, these challenges can be solved with minor adjustments to the existing proposal, yielding significant value without substantial effort.

6. Avoiding Irrelevant System Rebuilds

When organizations transition from legacy systems to modern platforms, they often seek to "upgrade" or "replace" their old system with newer technology. However, this can sometimes lead to the inadvertent rebuilding of an outdated solution.

Key Considerations

- **Reimagine the System:** Ensure that your proposed solution isn't just a technological upgrade of the legacy system. The goal is to build something more efficient, scalable, and future proof.

- **Modernization, Not Replication:** Focus on reimagining processes and improving them, rather than simply replicating old system features in a new environment.

CHAPTER 2   BUILDING A SUCCESSFUL SOLUTION ARCHITECT FRAMEWORK: KEY STAGES AND SKILLS

7. Conducting a SWOT Analysis

A **SWOT analysis** (Strengths, Weaknesses, Opportunities, and Threats) is a critical tool for assessing a solution's viability throughout its lifecycle. Periodically conducting a SWOT analysis allows you to evaluate your solution's effectiveness and identify potential risks or areas for improvement.

Key Considerations

- **Strengths:** What are the unique advantages of your solution? How does it align with customer goals and objectives?

- **Weaknesses:** What limitations exist within your solution? Could some aspects lead to future challenges, such as technical debt or lack of scalability?

- **Opportunities:** Are there opportunities for additional value? Could your solution address other customer pain points or create new business possibilities?

- **Threats:** What external factors might impact the success of your solution? Consider competition, market shifts, or technological changes that could undermine the proposal.

Summary

This module walks learners through the process of creating and proposing business solutions that are aligned with the client's needs and objectives. It covers the following key topics:

1. **Understanding the Business Needs:** Learning how to assess the client's current challenges and identify the underlying business needs

2. **Crafting the Solution:** Developing a technical solution that fits within the client's existing processes and systems while addressing their challenges

3. **Proposing the Solution:** Techniques for effectively presenting the solution to stakeholders, including decision-makers, and ensuring the proposal resonates with them

Effective Requirement Gathering: From Functional to Nonfunctional Needs

Introduction

The "Effective Requirement Gathering: From Functional to Nonfunctional Needs" module is designed to help professionals navigate the essential phase of requirements gathering in the context of project management and solution development. Having successfully moved past the presales phase, this module provides valuable insights into how to collect and work with both functional and nonfunctional requirements. While the methodology may vary across projects, this module offers a flexible approach that can be adapted to different project management frameworks, focusing on the core techniques and best practices for effective requirement gathering.

Leading Requirement Capture Sessions

The solution architect plays a critical role in leading requirement capture sessions, transforming high-level customer needs into implementable requirements. It is essential for the solution architect to be well-informed before the first session to ensure productive discussions. This information should drive the session's focus, even if they weren't involved in the presales phase.

Effective requirement gathering requires flexibility. While it's important to have a clear plan and templates for the session, the solution architect should remain adaptable to the specific needs of the project and customer. Rigid adherence to methodology may stifle creativity, so a balance should be maintained between structure and openness to new ideas.

What a Requirement Looks Like

A requirement should address the fundamental elements of who, what, and why. These parameters should be documented in a manner that is testable and accountable, such as user stories or line-item requirements. Larger requirements should be broken down into manageable components. In agile methodologies, these are often referred to as epics. The solution architect must ensure that requirements are divided into smaller, actionable parts.

Prioritization

Prioritizing requirements is a critical task, given the limited time and resources available for a project. The solution architect, in collaboration with the project team and customer, should prioritize the requirements list or backlog. The concept of a Minimum Viable Product (MVP) is often used, focusing on the requirements necessary for initial deployment. The remaining requirements are scheduled for future iterations or sprints. By aligning prioritization with key business objectives, the solution architect ensures that critical business needs are addressed first. This approach helps identify any disconnects between the requirements and the objectives.

Feasibility

Before proceeding with the implementation of requirements, the solution architect must assess their feasibility. If requirements are not achievable due to factors like data unavailability or system limitations, they should be flagged. A critical question to ask during this phase is: "Is there anything that would prevent these requirements from being completed?"

Managing Attendees

Setting expectations ahead of the sessions is crucial to ensure that the right stakeholders are involved. The solution architect should invite experienced individuals who understand the key areas under discussion. Multiple, smaller sessions focused on specific parts of the process can be more effective than large, general sessions. Having relevant people in the room helps provide a complete understanding of the process and avoids unnecessary follow-up for missing information.

While inviting senior management can be beneficial for decisive inputs, their presence may cause lower-level attendees to defer to them, reducing the quality of information gathered. The solution architect should manage this dynamic carefully, addressing any issues as they arise.

Prework Before Sessions

Preparation is vital for leading a successful requirement gathering session. The solution architect should gather as much information as possible about the existing solution and its processes. This includes reviewing any materials collected by the presales team to avoid redundant information. If demo recordings exist, reviewing them can also help the solution architect become better informed prior to the sessions.

CHAPTER 2   BUILDING A SUCCESSFUL SOLUTION ARCHITECT FRAMEWORK: KEY STAGES AND SKILLS

Driving Toward Requirement Clarity

Often, the initial statement of a requirement is vague or incomplete. The solution architect must engage in investigative work to clarify the true underlying need. Asking "Why?" is a critical technique for understanding the core issue, but it should be done tactfully to avoid offending users. For example, instead of simply accepting a broad requirement, the solution architect might ask questions like "Can you walk me through a typical day for this process?" or "Who else is involved in this process?"

By asking open-ended questions, the solution architect can refine the requirement and ensure that it is well understood. It's important to guide the discussion to a point where the requirement is clear and actionable, as demonstrated in the example of refining a report requirement to focus on expired transactions over $50,000.

Resolving Conflicting Requirements

Conflicting requirements from different stakeholders are common. The solution architect must remain neutral while guiding the team toward a resolution. Offering solutions or compromises can help, but the architect should avoid getting involved in corporate politics. Their focus should be on aligning the requirements with the solution vision.

Standing Up for Your Perspective

At times, the solution architect must push back on certain requirements. This involves respectfully communicating the solution vision and demonstrating how it aligns with the customer's goals. It's essential to be assertive without being dismissive of the customer's ideas, ensuring that the solution architect's recommendations are framed as solutions to the customer's problems rather than as a critique of their needs.

Identifying Functional Requirements

Functional requirements define the behaviors and functionalities that a solution must exhibit. They describe what the system should do and how users interact with it. These requirements should be clear and concise and capture the who, what, and why of each action. If a requirement is too large, it should be broken down into smaller, more manageable parts.

Example of Functional Requirements

Here are some examples of well-defined functional requirements:

- As a sales user, I need to be able to close an opportunity as lost and then capture why it was lost so that we can improve our sales tactics in the future.

- As a sales manager, I need to be able to approve a discount on a quote so that I can reduce the total price and give a discount to the customer.

- As a staff accountant, I want to be prevented from closing a batch that has pending items so that I do not have to reopen it later.

These examples clearly capture the user, the action they need to perform, and the reason behind it, offering a clear understanding of the requirement.

Poorly Worded Requirements

- Opportunities can be won or lost.
- Price should reflect discounts.

CHAPTER 2   BUILDING A SUCCESSFUL SOLUTION ARCHITECT FRAMEWORK: KEY STAGES AND SKILLS

- From the Batch Item list, selecting the Close Batch button, which is the third button from the left, should close the batch if no items exist that would stop it from happening.

These requirements are vague and don't specify the "who," "what," or "why," making them harder to implement and test.

Mapping to Process

When gathering functional requirements, it's often more effective to map them to specific business processes rather than just listing individual features or functions. Creating user stories or process diagrams can help convey the complete user journey and illustrate how the system will be used in practice. This method helps ensure that the requirements align with real-world needs, and it serves as a basis for breaking down tasks into smaller, actionable items during the planning phase.

Acceptance Criteria

For each functional requirement, clear acceptance criteria must be defined to specify how the requirement will be considered complete or "satisfied." These criteria are critical for testing and validation, and they help prevent misunderstandings about the scope of the requirement. Reviewing acceptance criteria with stakeholders ensures accuracy and can help prevent scope creep. It is also essential for identifying requirements that might be unrealistic and negotiating compromises that are achievable. To create, manage, and maintain requirements, you could use Azure DevOps, which includes the following features:

- **Azure Boards:** Manage requirements as **Epics**, **Features**, **User Stories**, and **Tasks**
- **Work Items:** Capture functional requirements, business rules, and acceptance criteria
- **Backlogs and Sprints:** Prioritize and plan development cycles
- **Test Plans:** Link requirements with test cases for validation
- **Integration:** Works seamlessly with Power Platform ALM (Application Lifecycle Management)

Capture Exceptions

When documenting requirements, it is important to capture potential exceptions to the standard workflow. While most requirements will have a straightforward path, there are often exceptional scenarios that should be addressed. These exceptions may require additional procedures, but they should not dominate the design process. It is equally important to assess how frequently these exceptions occur, as frequent exceptions may require changes to business processes or software customization.

Avoiding Scope Creep

Scope creep is the gradual expansion of the project scope beyond the original plan, which can lead to budget overruns and project delays. The solution architect must be vigilant in identifying requirements that are out of scope and manage them appropriately. Any out-of-scope requirements should be assessed through the project governance process, and decisions should be made whether to accept them, potentially resulting in a change order, or reject them. Ignoring scope creep can have significant negative impacts on a project's success.

Identifying Nonfunctional Requirements

Nonfunctional requirements (NFRs) are essential for ensuring that a system operates efficiently and securely and meets operational and performance standards. Unlike functional requirements, which describe specific tasks and behaviors of a system, nonfunctional requirements focus on how the system performs and the constraints under which it operates.

These requirements may have dependencies on external factors, such as hardware, network infrastructure, or regulatory constraints. These dependencies can influence project timelines and overall feasibility. Identifying these dependencies early on is critical to prevent delays or misunderstandings about the system's capabilities.

Common Nonfunctional Requirement Types

1. **Availability**

   Ensures the system is available and functional when users need it

   Example: "The system must be available 99.9% of the time during business hours (9 AM–6 PM, Monday to Friday)."

2. **Compliance/Regulatory**

   Ensures that the system meets relevant industry standards, regulations, or legal requirements
   Example: "The application must comply with GDPR standards for data storage and user privacy."

3. **Data Retention/Residency**

   Specifies how long data must be stored and where it can be physically located, ensuring compliance with data protection regulations

Example: "Customer transaction data must be retained for seven years and stored within the European Union."

4. **Performance (e.g., Response Time)**

   Describes the acceptable speed and responsiveness of the system

   Example: "The system should return search results within two seconds for up to 100 concurrent users."

5. **Privacy**

   Specifies how sensitive data will be protected and how user privacy will be ensured

   Example: "All customer personal data must be encrypted both at rest and in transit."

6. **Recovery Time**

   Specifies how quickly the system must recover from an outage or disaster

   Example: "The system must be recoverable within one hour of a disaster event."

7. **Security**

   Outlines the security measures required to protect the system and its data from unauthorized access or breaches

   Example: "All user accounts must have multifactor authentication enabled."

CHAPTER 2   BUILDING A SUCCESSFUL SOLUTION ARCHITECT FRAMEWORK: KEY STAGES AND SKILLS

8. **Scalability**

    Defines how the system should scale to handle increased loads without performance degradation

    Example: "The system should scale to support 1000 concurrent users without performance issues."

Examples of well-written nonfunctional requirements:

1. **Performance**

    - "Average screen load time for internal users not on mobile should be under three seconds."

2. **Scalability**

    - "The system should be able to handle up to 100 concurrent users submitting cases on the external portal without performance degradation."

3. **Recovery Time**

    - "The system must be able to recover from any failure within one hour and restore data from the last backup."

Examples of poorly written nonfunctional requirements:

1. "All screens in the app should load as fast as possible."

    - This is vague, as "fast as possible" is subjective and lacks a measurable target.

2. "The external portal must be able to handle peak traffic."

    - This requirement is not specific, as "peak traffic" is undefined, and no performance metrics are provided.

3. "The system must be recoverable after a disaster."

    - While the recovery aspect is addressed, this requirement does not specify the recovery time or process.

Feasibility of Nonfunctional Requirements

When formulating nonfunctional requirements, it is essential to consider the feasibility of meeting those requirements, given the project's budget and resources. For instance, specifying a system uptime of 99.999% might be difficult to achieve if the current system can only support 99.9% availability. Balancing high standards with realistic resource allocation ensures that nonfunctional requirements are achievable and aligned with the project's goals.

Measuring Compliance

Nonfunctional requirements must specify how compliance will be measured to ensure that they are being met. For instance:

- **Performance:** Define whether the response time of two seconds applies only to internal users or includes mobile users as well.
- **Availability:** If uptime is stated as 99.9%, define the measurement window (e.g., monthly uptime).

Clearly outlining the measurement methods helps avoid confusion and ensures that performance expectations are met.

Potential concerns for your project:

- **Hardware and Network Dependencies:** If the client uses outdated hardware or has limited network bandwidth, it may affect the performance of the system, especially for requirements like response time or scalability.

- **Legacy Applications:** Clients with older systems may not support modern browser technologies, impacting system performance and usability.

- **External Dependencies:** External factors such as Internet security software, firewalls, or compliance officers can affect security and privacy requirements.

Finalizing Requirements: A Step-by-Step Review Process

Once the requirements collection phase is complete, it's critical for the solution architect to review and finalize the requirements. This review ensures that all requirements align with the project's goals, are feasible, and are clearly understood by all stakeholders. The process involves checking for completeness, accuracy, scope, priorities, and alignment with business objectives.

Key Questions to Ask During the Requirements Review

1. **Are the Requirements Complete?**
    - **Who needs the requirements and why do they need them?**

Ensure that the requirements are comprehensive and cater to the needs of all stakeholders involved, such as end users, business owners, technical teams, and compliance officers.

- **Have all user needs been captured?**

    Confirm that all relevant functionality, performance, and operational aspects are covered.

2. **Is the Estimate Adequate?**

    - **Did details change, or are any revisions required?**

        Verify if any changes occurred in the requirements after the initial collection phase and assess whether any details need adjustments.

    - **Is the time, cost, and resource estimate sufficient?**

        Review whether the initial estimates for time and resources are realistic based on the scope and complexity of the finalized requirements.

3. **Is the Priority Correct?**

    - **Does the priority seem too low or too high?**

        Assess if the priority of each requirement is appropriately set, ensuring critical features are prioritized and non-essential tasks are marked as lower priority. This helps guide development efforts effectively.

4. **Is Everything in Scope?**

    - **Was any important requirement overlooked?**

        Double-check if any essential requirements were inadvertently excluded and need to be included within the defined scope.

    - **Are there any out-of-scope items?**

        Make sure that any requirements outside of the project's defined scope are identified and handled appropriately, ensuring they don't inadvertently impact the project's schedule or budget.

5. **Have the Requirements Mapped to Business Objectives?**

    - **How can requirements that don't map be dealt with?**

        Confirm that each requirement aligns with the overall business goals and objectives. If any requirement doesn't contribute directly to the objectives, assess whether it should be modified or excluded. Ensure that every requirement has clear business value.

6. **Have the Stakeholders Reached an Agreement on the Plan?**

    - **Are all stakeholders aligned with the finalized requirements?**

        Ensure that the stakeholders (such as business leaders, technical teams, end users, and others) have reviewed and agreed on the plan. This helps ensure no discrepancies in expectations later in the project.

CHAPTER 2   BUILDING A SUCCESSFUL SOLUTION ARCHITECT FRAMEWORK: KEY STAGES AND SKILLS

7. **Does a Roadmap to the Next Iteration Exist?**

    - **Is there a roadmap for the next iteration of the project?**

        Define clear milestones for the next iteration or sprint, ensuring that development can proceed in manageable phases with clear objectives.

    - **Is there a roadmap for the entire solution?**

        Map out the long-term roadmap for the entire solution. This includes the overarching goals, major deliverables, and timelines for the full project lifecycle, guiding the team through multiple iterations.

Additional Considerations for Finalizing Requirements

- **Document All Requirements Clearly:** Ensure that each requirement is documented in a clear, unambiguous manner to avoid misunderstandings during development.

- **Create an Approval Process:** Engage all stakeholders in a formal review and approval process for the finalized requirements, ensuring that there is consensus before moving forward.

- **Prepare for Change:** Acknowledge that requirements can evolve during the project lifecycle. Have a process in place to accommodate changes, track them, and assess their impact on the project.

- **Validate with Real-World Scenarios:** Validate requirements by considering how they will perform in real-world scenarios, identifying potential bottlenecks or challenges early on.

Assessing and Refining Requirements

Introduction to Fit-Gap Analysis

A fit-gap analysis helps you identify the differences between your defined requirements and the current or proposed solution. It highlights areas where the solution falls short, allowing you to address those gaps effectively. To perform a successful fit-gap analysis, it's crucial to have a thorough understanding of the requirements and a clear view of the components in your proposed solution. How you handle the identified gaps depends on various factors, such as time, budget, and available resources. These factors are often represented in the trade-off triangle, which includes **scope**, **resources**, and **schedule**. The rule of the triangle is straightforward: when one side changes, at least one other side must adjust accordingly.

In this module, you will learn to *explore the feasibility of requirements*, *refine requirements based on proof-of-concept insights*, *conduct a fit-gap analysis*, *evaluate Dynamics 365 applications to meet requirements*, *review third-party applications*, and *leverage alternate solutions* to address unmet needs.

Determining the Feasibility of Requirements

Feasibility is a fundamental aspect of the requirement gathering and fit-gap analysis process. As new details and perspectives arise, it's essential to regularly reassess the feasibility of each requirement. What seemed possible or reasonable at the outset may no longer hold up once more information or constraints come to light. Requirements that pose feasibility challenges should be revisited with subject matter experts for deeper insights or potentially deprioritized based on their impact on the overall project.

Key Considerations for Feasibility

1. **Will People Use the Feature?**

    It's important to not only consider the technical aspects of a requirement but also its real-world utility for users. A feature might look great on paper, but if it doesn't align with the actual needs or behavior of users, it could fail to gain traction. For example, a fully automated process could reduce manual work but may be too rigid for common, dynamic situations, resulting in unnecessary rework. Additionally, a solution might solve a problem but use an overly complicated approach that could overwhelm the users or create a steeper learning curve. It's crucial to ensure that the feature is practical and accessible for the intended audience, considering their daily tasks and how they interact with technology.

2. **Is the Feature Technically Feasible?**

    Users often envision elaborate, customized solutions that may be beyond the current technical capabilities or platform limitations. During the fit-gap analysis, it's essential to evaluate if the requested solution can be realistically implemented within the technological framework available. Some requests might exceed the technical scope or require features that are not supported by the existing system. For example, if a process generates a high volume of requests, it could potentially overwhelm the platform's API, leading to performance issues or even system failure. Such considerations are vital in determining whether the feature is technically feasible or whether it needs to be simplified or reworked.

3. **Is the Process Feasible or Overlooked?**

    Sometimes, individual requirements don't directly highlight the business process they affect, but when considered collectively, they can reveal an entire workflow that needs to be evaluated. It's crucial to review the requirements to identify any business processes that may have been overlooked. Furthermore, ensure that any processes that might seem obvious are assessed for practicality. For instance, a sales process could appear straightforward, but once you review it thoroughly, you might discover that certain exceptions or special cases need to be accounted for. These could impact the feasibility of the process, and failure to consider them could lead to bottlenecks or inefficiencies down the line.

4. **Do Regulatory Rules or Laws Restrict the Requirement?**

    In regulated industries, certain requirements may inadvertently conflict with legal or regulatory standards. During the requirement gathering phase, it's easy to get caught up in the excitement of what's possible from a business or technological standpoint. However, it's essential to involve experts who understand the regulatory landscape and verify that the proposed solution complies with relevant laws, such as data protection regulations, industry standards, or safety protocols. If a requirement doesn't adhere to these standards, it may be legally unfeasible, even though it seems beneficial from an operational perspective. Addressing these concerns early helps prevent costly delays or rework later in the project.

By taking the time to reflect on the feasibility of each requirement, you ensure that your solution is both practical and achievable. Reassessing the feasibility during the fit-gap analysis or design phase allows you to adjust, reprioritize, and streamline requirements to match the reality of the available resources, technology, and regulatory constraints. This helps avoid surprises during implementation and ensures a smoother, more successful project outcome.

Learn from a Proof of Concept (PoC)

A proof of concept (PoC) is an essential step in the solution development lifecycle, particularly when working with platforms like Dynamics 365 and Power Platform. The primary goal of a PoC is to validate an idea, test assumptions, and ensure the feasibility of a solution before fully investing in development. It allows stakeholders to evaluate whether the proposed solution will meet business requirements, operate within the technical environment, and deliver the desired user experience.

The PoC phase serves as a practical demonstration, often focusing on a small, manageable portion of the overall solution. By testing specific features or processes, a PoC helps identify potential challenges early in the project. This provides an opportunity to adjust design, address technical issues, and refine user interactions before committing to a large-scale rollout. A well-executed PoC can save time and resources by revealing issues that might not be apparent in the planning or requirement gathering phase.

Key insights from a PoC include

1. **Feasibility Check:** It helps determine whether the proposed solution is technically and operationally feasible. This includes testing the platform's capabilities, integrations, and scalability.

2. **User Experience Evaluation:** By involving end users early, a PoC helps assess if the solution aligns with their needs and workflows. Feedback from users can be used to refine the design to ensure better usability.

3. **Business Alignment:** A PoC ensures that the solution addresses business requirements effectively and supports key processes, offering stakeholders the confidence that the project is on the right track.

4. **Risk Mitigation:** Early testing reduces the risk of major setbacks or failures later in the project, as issues can be detected and addressed early.

5. **Feedback Loop:** It provides valuable feedback from key stakeholders, enabling continuous refinement and improvement of the solution before large-scale implementation.

A PoC is a critical phase that helps ensure the project stays aligned with business goals, user expectations, and technical feasibility. It mitigates risk, saves costs, and ensures a more successful final product.

… CHAPTER 2 BUILDING A SUCCESSFUL SOLUTION ARCHITECT FRAMEWORK: KEY STAGES AND SKILLS

Categorizing Business Requirements and Performing Fit-Gap Analysis

Fit-gap analysis is a crucial process to identify the discrepancies between business requirements and the current or proposed solution. It helps in sizing, prioritizing, and addressing gaps in a structured manner. The main goal is to evaluate whether a business requirement can be met using existing functionality, or if it requires additional customization or configuration. As a solution architect, conducting a fit-gap analysis allows you to ensure that you're using available tools effectively while also avoiding unnecessary custom development that could complicate the solution.

In the context of business applications like Dynamics 365, which come with a variety of built-in functionalities, a fit-gap analysis helps identify what can be achieved using out-of-the-box features and where custom solutions are needed. The analysis process can range from a mental evaluation for smaller projects to more detailed documentation using tools like Excel templates or Azure DevOps. The essential part of the process is the value derived from the output of the analysis.

Key Steps to Perform Fit-Gap Analysis

1. **Severity of the Gap or Category**

    - **Fit:** This category indicates that the current out-of-the-box functionality in the system meets the requirement. No additional customization or configuration is necessary.

    - **Configured:** This refers to requirements that can be fulfilled by configuring existing features, such as changing settings, workflows, or reports, without needing custom development.

- **Custom:** This category includes requirements that cannot be met through standard features and require custom development or third-party tools.

- **Other:** Some requirements may fall outside the typical fit or custom categories, such as external systems or special workflows that may require integration.

2. **Level of Effort:** The level of effort evaluates the amount of work required to close the identified gap. It can be categorized as low, medium, or high, or rated using a scale (e.g., 1–10). This step helps estimate the resources, time, and complexity involved in addressing the gap. Consistency in the rating system is crucial to track and compare efforts accurately.

3. **Priority:** Priority levels indicate the importance of addressing each gap. Business priorities often drive this, but the solution architect should also consider technical dependencies and the foundation of the architecture. Some gaps might need to be prioritized higher to ensure the stability and scalability of the solution.

4. **Implementation Notes:** This section provides high-level descriptions of how the gap can be addressed, helping to guide the team in closing the gap. These notes should not be highly detailed design specifications but rather a summary of the required steps or assumptions made during the analysis. For instance, adding an N:1 relationship in the data model could be enough to indicate a configuration requirement, which will inform the overall implementation strategy.

Evaluate Dynamics 365 and Microsoft Power Platform Apps

When developing a solution, it's important to determine whether to build it within **Dynamics 365** or the **Power Platform**. While both platforms offer robust capabilities, they are suited for different types of solutions, and in many cases, a solution will span across both. Understanding when to use a first-party Dynamics 365 app vs. leveraging Power Platform applications or external integrations is key to creating an effective solution. Experts in the field weigh in on best practices and considerations for making this choice.

Connectors and APIs

One of the biggest strengths of **Microsoft Power Platform** is the ability to use **connectors**. Connectors allow seamless integration with over 275 systems and services without needing to move your data. This capability supports **Power BI**, **Power Apps**, and **Power Automate**, enabling users to analyze, act on, and automate data across multiple services without migration. With **custom connectors**, users can extend this functionality to virtually any system with a REST API.

However, native **Dynamics 365 model-driven apps** do not directly support connectors. Instead, you can embed a **Power Apps Canvas app** into a Dynamics 365 app, allowing the use of connectors within that Canvas app. This integration brings external data into Dynamics 365 while keeping data within its original source, helping prevent unnecessary data migration.

Industry Accelerators and Common Data Model

The **Open Data Initiative** spearheaded by Microsoft, **Adobe**, and **SAP** has led to the development of the **Common Data Model** (CDM). The CDM standardizes business data across various Microsoft services, including ***Dynamics 365***, ***Power Apps***, ***Power BI***, and upcoming ***Azure data services***. By enabling interoperability across applications, the CDM allows a company's systems and vendors to work together more efficiently, using a common language for business entities. This enhances data consistency across sales, service, marketing, operations, finance, talent, and commerce.

To make the Common Data Model more relevant to specific industries, ***Microsoft*** is working on ***industry accelerators*** that provide tailored production-ready schemas. These accelerators cater to industries such as

- Banking
- Healthcare
- Education
- Nonprofit
- Automotive
- Media

These accelerators simplify the implementation process, allowing organizations in these industries to leverage prebuilt solutions that are customized for their specific needs.

AppSource

AppSource is Microsoft's marketplace where you can discover, try, and purchase apps that integrate with your Microsoft ecosystem. From ***Dynamics 365*** *to* ***Power BI***, users can find solutions that enhance their existing applications. Through **AppSource**, you can

- ***Discover the right app*** for your business needs
- ***Test apps for free*** before committing to a purchase

- **Reach a wider audience** by marketing your own services to over 100 million commercial active users

- **Enhance existing Microsoft investments**, improving what you already use in your business applications

AppSource enables organizations to expand their capabilities quickly and easily by adding specialized third-party apps that integrate seamlessly with Dynamics 365 and the Power Platform.

Summary

Fit-gap analysis is a critical process for assessing business requirements against available solutions, ensuring that existing features are leveraged before custom developments are considered. It involves identifying gaps, categorizing requirements, and prioritizing them to streamline solution design. The analysis helps determine the feasibility of each requirement, ensuring that the final solution is both practical and aligned with business goals.

By utilizing a proof of concept, businesses can validate requirements early, refine solutions, and reduce risks. In the case of Dynamics 365 and Power Platform, fit-gap analysis can be enhanced by leveraging built-in features, connectors, and APIs. These allow seamless integration with external systems and data sources, minimizing the need for data migration while maintaining a unified solution. The Common Data Model ensures data consistency across different applications and business processes, enabling smoother integrations.

For industry-specific solutions, accelerators provide ready-to-use schemas tailored to sectors like healthcare, banking, and education, facilitating quicker implementation. Additionally, AppSource offers a marketplace of third-party apps that can be integrated into Dynamics

365 and Power Platform, helping businesses extend functionality without reinventing the wheel. Overall, this approach ensures efficient, feasible, and scalable solutions that meet business needs while optimizing resources.

Conclusion: Building a Successful Solution Architect Framework

In this chapter, we've explored the fundamental stages and skills that are essential for building a successful Solution Architect framework. Becoming a proficient solution architect is a journey that requires a deep understanding of the path to mastery, from gaining technical expertise to developing strong business acumen and interpersonal skills. The customer discovery process is crucial in identifying the true needs and goals of clients, allowing architects to craft well-aligned and tailored solutions.

Crafting and proposing effective solutions involve combining creativity with technical knowledge to design systems that meet both functional and nonfunctional requirements. The ability to gather and assess these requirements—whether functional or nonfunctional—is vital to ensuring the solution is comprehensive and aligns with the client's objectives.

As we've highlighted, effective requirement gathering is a continuous process that doesn't just focus on what the system should do but also how it should perform under different conditions. By refining requirements and assessing their feasibility, a solution architect ensures that the final design will be practical, scalable, and sustainable.

Ultimately, success as a solution architect hinges on understanding the big picture while managing the intricate details of each project stage. Developing the right skill set and applying the right approach to each phase allow architects to deliver impactful and successful solutions that meet both the technical and business needs of their clients.

CHAPTER 3

Governance, Architecture, and Core Components in Power Platform and Dynamics 365

Chapter Goal: To equip readers with the knowledge to implement effective project governance frameworks, design scalable architectures, and leverage the capabilities of Power Apps and Power Automate to create enterprise-grade solutions. By the end of this chapter, readers will understand how governance, architecture, app development, and automation work cohesively to drive digital transformation.

Sub-topics:

1. Project Governance and Architecture in Power Platform and Dynamics 365
2. Exploring Power Apps and Automate

CHAPTER 3   GOVERNANCE, ARCHITECTURE, AND CORE COMPONENTS IN POWER
            PLATFORM AND DYNAMICS 365

Introduction

Success in Power Platform and Dynamics 365 implementations relies on a strong foundation of governance, architecture, and the effective use of its core components, Power Apps and Power Automate. Governance ensures projects align with business objectives, comply with regulations, and deliver value efficiently, while architecture sets the stage for scalable, secure, and high-performance solutions. At the same time, Power Apps empowers users to build tailored applications with minimal coding, and Power Automate simplifies workflows, reducing manual effort and enhancing productivity.

In this chapter, we'll explore how to establish project governance frameworks, define security and compliance policies, and design robust architectures. We'll also dive into Power Apps to uncover app-building techniques and explore how Power Automate facilitates process automation, both independently and as part of Dynamics 365 solutions. These interconnected elements will demonstrate how to unlock the full potential of the Power Platform for modern business challenges.

Project Governance in Power Platform and Dynamics 365

Introduction to Project Governance

As a solution architect for Microsoft Power Platform, your role is pivotal in steering a project's success. You're not just there to design technical solutions—you're also responsible for implementing governance, managing change processes, and keeping a close eye on project progress.

CHAPTER 3   GOVERNANCE, ARCHITECTURE, AND CORE COMPONENTS IN POWER PLATFORM AND DYNAMICS 365

Keeping Projects on Track

Take a moment to think about past projects you've been part of. Now, reflect on these questions:

- Did the project have a clear governance process?
- If it did, was that process consistently followed?
- Were risks identified, documented, and mitigated effectively?
- Was there a change control process in place?
- How effective were these processes, and how could they have been improved?

As a solution architect, these are the kinds of issues you'll frequently address. Before diving deeper into these topics, it's important to build a solid understanding of what project governance truly involves. Ready to explore? Let's dig in.

Project Governance: A Guide for Solution Architects

Alright, let's talk about project governance. You might be thinking, "Isn't that just project management?" Well, not quite. While there is some overlap, governance is a separate concept. It's the framework within which decisions about the project are made—essentially the decision-making process that guides your project. Without solid governance, you're setting yourself up for trouble.

Now, here's the thing: projects are dynamic. They're not static, and issues are bound to pop up. These could be minor hiccups at first, but if you ignore them, they can escalate and become major roadblocks. At the same time, if you spend too much time dwelling on each issue, you risk stalling the entire project. That's why having a good governance process is critical—it helps you tackle challenges as they arise, keeping the project moving forward.

So what's involved in governance? At its core, project governance is all about decision-making, and it boils down to three main questions:

1. **Authority:** Who's making the decisions? Do they have the expertise and experience to make the right calls? This is crucial for ensuring that the right people are at the helm, making informed decisions.

2. **Process:** How are decisions made? It's not just about deciding—it's about balancing the need for timely decisions with proper impact analysis. You want to act quickly but thoughtfully.

3. **Evidence:** What information do you need to decide? The data is key, but it's not just about having it—it's about analyzing it to understand the potential impact of your decisions.

Now, here's where it gets interesting. In a typical project, especially when you're working with Microsoft Power Platform, your customer (whether internal or external) might already have their own governance process in place. But let's be honest—these existing processes might not be fully aligned with the fast-paced nature of a Power Platform project. The decision-making speed and the level of detail required can be very different from what they're used to.

This is where the solution architect comes in. As a solution architect, you need to ensure that the governance process is tailored to meet the needs of a Microsoft Power Platform project. You might need to either tweak the existing governance process or, in some cases, build a new hybrid one that works best for your project's pace and complexity.

The Essentials of Governance

At the very least, here's what your project governance should cover:

- **Risks:** Document risks, evaluate them, and implement risk mitigation strategies.
- **Issues:** Log issues, evaluate them, and figure out how to address them.
- **Changes:** Track changes and have a formal change control process in place.

Remember, this isn't a detailed how-to on implementing governance. But the key takeaway is that as a solution architect, it's your responsibility to ensure that a governance process is in place that aligns with the unique needs of your project.

Reflecting on Your Experience

Think back to the projects you've worked on, and ask yourself:

- How were issues logged?
- Who had the authority to raise an issue?
- Were those issues evaluated properly? And by whom?
- How were changes raised, and was there a clear process for that?
- Were these processes appropriate for the scale and scope of your project?

Looking back, how could these processes have been improved to make the project run smoother? These are the questions you need to keep in mind as you shape the governance process for your Power Platform projects.

CHAPTER 3   GOVERNANCE, ARCHITECTURE, AND CORE COMPONENTS IN POWER PLATFORM AND DYNAMICS 365

Solution Architect's Role in Project Governance

Let's talk about your role as a solution architect in project governance. At first glance, it might seem like your main job is to handle all the issues and changes yourself, right? Well, that's not always the best approach. Yes, you have the expertise, but getting caught up in every change can slow things down. Especially in Microsoft Power Platform projects, things can change quickly, and it's easy to get stuck in the weeds, constantly monitoring those changes. Instead, your role should be to guide your team members in evaluating and analyzing issues and changes.

For many new solution architects, there's a shift from being the doer to becoming a leader who guides others. It's not always easy to step away from hands-on work, but your job is to empower your team to grow and handle things on their own.

Defining Governance with Microsoft Power Platform

In the context of Microsoft Power Platform, changes might be quick and easy to implement, but if you don't have a solid governance process in place, even small changes can cause major problems. As a solution architect, you need to make sure that the process for evaluating changes doesn't take longer than implementing them. It's all about balancing speed with proper analysis.

This is why your involvement in defining governance processes is crucial. You need to ensure that the governance procedures are well-suited to Power Platform technologies and don't create unnecessary overhead for your team.

Providing Actionable Feedback

As a solution architect, you're often the bridge between the customer and the team. You need to provide feedback to both sides, and that feedback must be actionable. Feedback starts from the very beginning—whether it's during the creation of the Request for Proposal (RFP) or Statement of Work (SOW)—and should continue throughout the project.

The key to feedback is making it constructive. It's easy to say, "This isn't working," but that's not helpful. Instead, offer a clear problem statement, explain why it's an issue, and outline the impact on the project. This helps everyone involved understand what needs to be done next.

Handling Bad News

Sometimes, you'll need to deliver bad news. And here's the thing: bad news doesn't get better with time. It's best to share it early so everyone can take appropriate action. Examples of bad news you shouldn't withhold:

- The cost of user licenses will increase by 87% if we move forward with that requirement.
- That feature is being deprecated.
- With the new relationship added, the data import will now take 30 days.
- The data migration has identified 200 new columns, and three new undocumented processes have emerged.

When delivering bad news, make sure it's actionable. Simply saying "Something's wrong" isn't helpful. Provide a clear problem statement, reference the issues, and explain how they impact the project.

CHAPTER 3   GOVERNANCE, ARCHITECTURE, AND CORE COMPONENTS IN POWER
            PLATFORM AND DYNAMICS 365

Helping Everyone Reach the Same Conclusion

As the solution architect, you might have the most experience, but it's not just about telling people what to do. You need to guide the team and customer to reach a consensus. Telling someone, "That won't work," will likely make them defensive. Instead, offer alternatives or help them see the bigger picture.

Ask leading questions like "Will this cause 1,000,000 Power Automate cloud flows to run with that configuration?" This makes them think about the broader impact of their decisions. The team might not have the full picture that you do, so it's your job to guide them toward the right solution.

Reviewing Work and Collaborating

A key part of your role is reviewing others' work. And while it might feel like you're doing the work yourself, reviewing is different—it's about providing guidance. If a design doesn't seem solid, encourage the creation of a proof of concept or other tests to validate the solution. You want to support the team in discovering the right answers.

The best solution architects don't hide behind their designs. They stay involved with the team, collaborate, and help solve problems together. Hiding behind your architecture designs or micromanaging won't get the job done. A successful solution architect is hands-on, guiding the team toward the project's vision.

Techniques for Keeping a Project on Track

As a solution architect, one of your most important responsibilities is ensuring that the project stays focused on its goals. You need to have practices in place that keep both the customer and your team informed about the project's progress and the challenges that may arise along the way.

Common Areas of Project Failure

A project can veer off track for many reasons, but some of the most common include

- **Not Documenting Assumptions:** If you don't document the assumptions made during the project, you risk misunderstandings down the line.

- **Not Conducting Risk Management:** Ignoring potential risks can derail the project when problems surface unexpectedly.

- **Excessive Analysis and Impact Assessment:** While analyzing impacts is important, too much analysis can lead to paralysis by analysis, delaying decisions.

- **Over-promising:** Overcommitting to deliverables that can't be realistically achieved is a recipe for failure.

- **Designing with Incorrect Assumptions or Requirements:** Starting with the wrong assumptions can result in a solution that doesn't meet the customer's needs.

- **Organizational Politics:** Internal team conflicts or politics can impede progress and cause delays.

- **Not Having Buy-in from Senior Management:** Without support from higher-ups, the project might not receive the necessary resources or direction.

- **Inability to Have a Complete Enterprise Vision:** Not seeing the bigger picture can lead to solutions that don't fit within the organization's overall strategy.

Of course, these aren't the only potential pitfalls. There are many factors that can cause a project to fail, but being aware of them up front will help you avoid them.

Characteristics of Successful Projects

Good projects don't just happen—they require careful planning and management. Successful projects typically have the following traits:

- **Knowing What a Finished Project Looks Like from the Customer's Perspective, Not Yours:** It's crucial to understand the customer's expectations and vision of success.

- **Having a Change Control Board to Manage Change:** This ensures changes are assessed, approved, and implemented in an organized manner.

- **Managing Risk Proactively:** Instead of waiting for risks to become problems, good projects anticipate and mitigate risks early.

- **Being More Agile:** Flexibility and the ability to adapt to changes as the project progresses is key.

- **Performing Project Checkpoints to Assess How You Are Doing:** Regular assessments help you stay on track and make adjustments if needed.

- **Having Retrospectives and Evaluating Lessons Learned:** Periodic evaluations provide valuable insights and opportunities for continuous improvement.

These characteristics, while not exhaustive, form the backbone of a successful project.

Project Checkpoints

One way to keep a project on track is by setting up clear checkpoints to measure progress. The solution architect should insist on regular progress reporting and have milestones at critical points in the project.

For example, a simple red, yellow, and green color-coding system can be used to assess the health of the project:

- **Red:** Indicates a significant issue that needs immediate attention.
- **Yellow:** Signals a potential issue that should be monitored and managed.
- **Green:** Everything is progressing as planned.

This simple system allows everyone involved to quickly gauge the project's health and identify areas requiring attention. While you don't have to use this exact system, the solution architect should agree on a straightforward health check process that everyone follows.

Retrospectives

As a solution architect, you must regularly assess how the project is progressing. Waiting until the end of the project to conduct a review isn't helpful because by then, it's too late to make adjustments. It's essential to gather feedback at regular intervals to address any issues early on.

Before each checkpoint, gather feedback from both inside and outside the project team. During the checkpoint meeting, focus on having no-fault discussions—creating a safe space where people can openly talk about what's working and what isn't. The goal is to learn from the feedback and set goals for the next checkpoint.

The idea is to turn any failures into actionable goals. By continuously assessing and adjusting, the project remains on course, and the team can continuously improve.

CHAPTER 3   GOVERNANCE, ARCHITECTURE, AND CORE COMPONENTS IN POWER PLATFORM AND DYNAMICS 365

Power Platform Architecture

Introduction

As a solution architect for Microsoft Power Platform, you're responsible for designing solutions that leverage its powerful capabilities. Understanding how the platform is structured, its components, and its limits is key to building effective solutions.

When you design a solution, it's crucial to grasp the various components and capabilities of Microsoft Power Platform, as these will shape how you approach your design.

Microsoft Power Platform Components

Microsoft Power Platform is a low-code, fast application development platform. It consists of several independent but closely related tools that work together to help you build powerful solutions:

- **Microsoft Power Apps:** This tool allows anyone to create custom web and mobile apps using low-code or no-code methods. It empowers users to build apps without needing to know much about coding.

- **Microsoft Power Automate:** A cloud-based workflow tool that connects cloud and desktop apps to automate business processes. With Power Automate, you can streamline repetitive tasks and integrate various apps seamlessly.

- **Microsoft Power BI:** A self-service analytics tool that helps users gain insights from their data. With Power BI, you can create models, reports, and dashboards that visualize your data, allowing businesses to make informed decisions.

CHAPTER 3   GOVERNANCE, ARCHITECTURE, AND CORE COMPONENTS IN POWER PLATFORM AND DYNAMICS 365

- **Microsoft Power Virtual Agents:** This tool lets you create chatbots without writing a single line of code, all from a user-friendly browser interface.

- **Microsoft Power Pages:** With Power Pages, users can create websites that are accessible to people outside the organization. These sites can allow users to view and interact with data stored in Dataverse.

These tools form the core of Microsoft Power Platform and are designed to work together in harmony.

In addition to these tools, there are other key components that help support and enhance your solutions:

- **Microsoft Dataverse:** A no-code platform that allows you to create tables, define relationships, and implement business logic.

- **Data Connectors:** These connectors enable Microsoft Power Platform tools to access various data sources and services, from Office 365 to third-party services like Twitter, Dropbox, and Mailchimp.

- **AI Builder:** A suite of AI model types that use data stored in Dataverse to create, train, and deploy machine learning models. These can be integrated with other Power Platform tools to add intelligence to your apps.

CHAPTER 3 GOVERNANCE, ARCHITECTURE, AND CORE COMPONENTS IN POWER PLATFORM AND DYNAMICS 365

Cloud-Based Solution

Microsoft Power Platform is a cloud-based Software-as-a-Service (SaaS) solution. It's hosted within a Microsoft Entra ID tenant, licensed through Microsoft 365, and secured using Microsoft Entra ID. Running on Microsoft Azure, the platform is scalable and globally available, ensuring high availability and performance.

Microsoft Power Platform Capabilities

While each component of Microsoft Power Platform provides powerful capabilities on its own, they become even more impactful when combined. Here's how the various tools interact and complement each other:

- **Power Apps:** Enables users to take action on data and automate business processes
- **Power Automate:** Automates apps, performing tasks on behalf of the user in response to events or triggers
- **Power BI:** Analyzes data captured by apps, offering insights and visualizations
- **Power Virtual Agents:** Assists users with chatbots for support or process automation
- **Power Pages:** Connects to external users through websites

Moreover, these tools can integrate further:

- Power Automate flows can be triggered from Power Apps, Power Virtual Agents, and Power BI alerts.
- Power BI dashboards and tiles can be embedded within Power Apps.
- Power Apps can be integrated into Power BI dashboards.

This interconnected ecosystem enables seamless solutions that empower businesses to automate processes, visualize data, and engage with users effectively.

The Role of Data

Data is at the heart of everything in Microsoft Power Platform. By using connectors, you can access data where it resides, or you can store your data in **Microsoft Dataverse**, a powerful platform for building business apps. The connectors allow you to link Microsoft Power Platform to

- **Office 365 services** like SharePoint and email
- **Azure services**, including Azure SQL
- **Non-Microsoft services** such as Twitter, SendGrid, Dropbox, and Mailchimp

Microsoft Dataverse offers more than just data storage—it controls security, implements logic, and enables integrations. It provides a rich set of features that allow you to create sophisticated, scalable business solutions.

Accessing Dataverse Through Environments

Before diving into the details of how Dataverse functions, it's important to first understand how it is accessed through **environments**. Environments help organize your data and solutions, and they play a crucial role in managing security and governance within Microsoft Power Platform.

Environments

An environment is a space where your organization's business data, apps, and workflows are stored, managed, and shared. Administrators can create and control access to environments, ensuring that the right users have the right level of access to the right resources.

CHAPTER 3   GOVERNANCE, ARCHITECTURE, AND CORE COMPONENTS IN POWER PLATFORM AND DYNAMICS 365

An environment includes several key components:

- **Name:** The environment's name for identification
- **Location:** The Azure region where the environment's data, apps, and flows are stored
- **Admins:** The users who can manage the environment
- **Security Group:** Defines who can access the environment
- **Apps:** The applications created within the environment
- **Flows:** The workflows created in the environment using Power Automate
- **Bots:** Chatbots created within the environment using Power Virtual Agents
- **Connectors:** Custom connectors integrated into the environment for accessing external data
- **Gateways:** On-premises gateways connected to the environment for hybrid solutions
- **Dataverse (Optional):** The optional database instance used for storing business data

Environments act as containers to manage all these assets and help control who can access them, ensuring that each user has the appropriate permissions.

Tenants

In the Microsoft 365 ecosystem, a **Microsoft Entra ID tenant** is used for authentication and authorization. You don't need a separate Azure subscription to access **Microsoft Entra ID**; it's included with your Microsoft 365 subscription. Adding a user to Microsoft 365 automatically adds them to the Microsoft Entra ID portal.

Each Microsoft Entra ID tenant is located in a specific Azure region, usually the region where the tenant was first created. **Environments** are built within a Microsoft Entra ID tenant, and access to them is controlled by **Microsoft Entra ID**.

Multiple Environments

You can have multiple environments within your organization, and the way you organize them depends on your specific needs. Here are some examples of how you might structure multiple environments:

- You might choose to create only one environment to host all your apps and data.

- You could create separate environments for testing and production versions of your apps.

- You may want separate environments for different teams or departments, each containing relevant apps and data for their specific needs.

- In large organizations with multiple branches or global offices, you might create different environments for each region.

Environments provide a scope for lifecycle management and permissions, helping you organize and control access to your resources.

Items Not Contained in Environments

While environments store many Microsoft Power Platform components, not everything related to your solution is contained within an environment. For example:

- **Power BI** workspaces, datasets, reports, and dashboards are not part of an environment.

- **Azure services** you deploy are not contained in environments.

- **Non-customer engagement Dynamics 365 apps** (like Finance or Business Central) are also separate from environments.

You need to consider how to manage access to these external components when designing your solution.

Security Layers

Microsoft Power Platform employs multiple layers of security to ensure the safety of your data:

- **Microsoft Entra ID:** User authentication and identity management is handled by Microsoft Entra ID. With this, you can enforce security policies like multifactor authentication (MFA) and single sign-on (SSO) to simplify access.

- **Licensing:** Users need appropriate licenses to access Microsoft Power Platform tools and features.

- **Environments:** Access to environments is controlled by Microsoft Entra ID security groups, ensuring that only authorized users can access the environment.

- **Data Loss Prevention Policies:** These policies restrict the use of connectors and help prevent data leakage by limiting the flow of data across environments.

- **Security Roles:** Permissions to tables and data rows in Dataverse are managed via security roles, ensuring that only authorized users can access specific data.

- **Encryption:** All data is encrypted at rest using SQL Server Transparent Data Encryption (TDE) and encrypted in transit using SSL. IT, data security, and administration teams are responsible for defining and enforcing the DLP, compliance, and security controls and reviewing them every 30–90 days to keep data secure.

Environment Data Location

Microsoft operates a global network of data centers that support Microsoft Power Platform across **17 different locations**, offering organizations the flexibility to meet data residency, sovereignty, and compliance requirements.

When creating an environment, you get to choose its geographical location. The environment's data will be stored in the selected region. It's important to choose the right location from the start, as it is possible to relocate an environment, but it's easier to get it right initially.

Regions

Microsoft provides three main types of cloud deployments:

- **Global Cloud:** This is a public Internet deployment that gives you access to globally connected cloud services. The global clouds include regions in the **United States**, **Europe**, and **Asia Pacific**.

- **Local Cloud:** This option meets local data residency requirements, ensuring that all data stays within the designated country or region. Examples include **Canada**, **Brazil**, **United Kingdom**, **France**, **Germany**, **India**, **Japan**, **Australia**, **United Arab Emirates**, **Switzerland**, **and South Africa**.

- **Sovereign Cloud:** For the strictest compliance and sovereignty standards, data stays entirely within the country or region of residence. Sovereign clouds include the **US Government** and **China**.

Microsoft is always expanding, so new regions may be added over time. Keep an eye on availability for the latest locations.

Data Residency

Choosing the right environment location depends on several factors:

- Are users spread out across different regions?
- What level of latency is acceptable for your applications?
- Does your organization have separate autonomous business units with separate data that cannot be shared?
- Are there specific features required in a region?
- Do you have security and compliance requirements to consider?

In general, it's best to choose a location that is geographically close to the users who will access the data, unless there are other constraints that demand a different setup.

Compliance and Data Protection

When deciding on a location for your environment, regulatory and compliance requirements such as **GDPR** must be considered.

Microsoft does not transfer customer data outside of the selected geographic region unless it's required for **customer support**, troubleshooting, or to comply with **legal obligations**.

For globally stored information like user identities, Microsoft Power Platform keeps such data in a US-based data center. All customer data and geo-redundant copies are stored within the chosen **geo**.

When to Use Multiple Environments

Creating multiple environments can help in various situations, including

- **Managing Application Lifecycle:** For example, separating **Development**, **Test**, and **Production** environments

- **Isolating Resources:** Keeping resources separate for different user groups or markets

- **Supporting Regulatory Requirements:** Ensuring compliance with legal or regional constraints

- **Experimentation:** Creating dedicated environments where makers can try out new ideas without affecting production

Managed Environments

Managed Environments enhance governance capabilities, making it easier to manage Microsoft Power Platform at scale. Once an environment is enabled as managed, you can

- **Limit Sharing:** Restrict how widely Canvas apps can be shared, reducing risk.

- **View Usage Insights:** Gain insights into how the environment is being used through weekly email digests.

- **Control Data Policies:** Limit the connectors available in the environment.

- **Set Up Power Platform Pipelines:** Easily deploy solutions between environments.

Landing Zones

Power Platform Landing Zones is a reference architecture and methodology to guide organizations in setting up and managing environments at scale. It provides a structured approach to building environments based on design principles that align with Power Platform's roadmap and best practices for security, governance, and compliance.

Connecting to On-Premises Networks

In some cases, organizations may require a **secure connection** between on-premises systems and Power Platform services. Here are a couple of options:

- **Azure ExpressRoute:** This offers private connectivity between your on-premises network and Microsoft cloud services, ensuring that customer data does not travel over the public Internet.

- **On-Premises Data Gateway:** For accessing on-premises data sources, the gateway allows you to connect Power Platform apps and flows securely to your internal systems.

CHAPTER 3   GOVERNANCE, ARCHITECTURE, AND CORE COMPONENTS IN POWER PLATFORM AND DYNAMICS 365

These options ensure compliance and reliable data transfer between your on-premises and cloud environments.

Data Accessing and Storing

1. **Connectors**

    - **Purpose:** Connectors enable integration with various data sources and services, allowing Power Apps, Power Automate, and Power BI to access and manipulate data without moving it.

    - **Functionality:** Over 400 prebuilt connectors are available, and custom connectors can be created if necessary.

    - **Data Locations:** Connectors work with both cloud-based and on-premises data through gateways.

2. **Dataverse**

    - **Storage:** Dataverse is the recommended data storage option for new data stores or when using Power Platform features like AI Builder or Power Apps portals.

    - **Capabilities:** Dataverse is more than just a database; it includes built-in functionality for security, business logic, data validation, and event integration.

    - **Security:** Supports role-based, column-level, and row-level security, ensuring granular access control.

3. **APIs**
    - Power Platform uses REST APIs to interact with data and manage resources, making it easier for custom logic integration and interaction with external services.
    - APIs support OData, allowing for easy consumption of data across platforms.

Key Features and Benefits of Microsoft Dataverse

1. **Data Security**
    - Role-based access controls and security at both the column and row levels ensure that only authorized users can access sensitive data.
    - Integrates seamlessly with Microsoft Entra ID for identity and access management.

2. **Custom Business Logic**
    - Dataverse allows for automation and validation of business logic using tools like business rules, workflows, calculated columns, and Power Automate integrations.

3. **Simplified Data Management**
    - Dataverse abstracts the complexities of underlying storage, providing a unified and scalable data storage solution with global availability.

4. **Integration with Other Systems**

    - Dataverse supports integration with a wide range of systems via APIs, including external tools like Xamarin for customer-facing applications.

    - Microsoft Azure Cognitive Search enables powerful data search capabilities.

5. **Virtual Tables**

    - Virtual tables in Dataverse allow you to access external data without physically moving it, making it easier to integrate data from various systems, including SharePoint and SQL Server.

Extensibility and Customization

1. **Custom Connectors and APIs**

    - When prebuilt connectors do not meet specific needs, you can create custom connectors or define your own APIs to integrate with any service that supports REST API.

    - Custom connectors and APIs are essential for creating complex workflows or managing business logic tailored to your organization.

2. **Developer Support**

    - Dataverse provides an extensibility model that includes a rich API, support for client-side scripting (TypeScript/JavaScript), and integration with Azure services like Service Bus and Event Hubs.

- These features allow developers to extend functionality and integrate with other business systems more effectively.

3. **Custom Logic**
   - In addition to business rules and workflows, developers can use custom actions and APIs to bundle operations into single calls, simplifying the process of creating complex workflows.

Considerations for Solution Architects

As a solution architect, understanding how to effectively leverage the capabilities of Dataverse and connectors is crucial for designing scalable, secure, and maintainable solutions. It's important to

- Investigate whether prebuilt connectors meet your needs or if custom connectors are necessary
- Take advantage of Dataverse's security and extensibility features to build robust and efficient solutions
- Ensure smooth integration with external systems and APIs through tools like Virtual Table connectors

By effectively using Dataverse and connectors, businesses can seamlessly integrate data from multiple sources, automate processes, and gain valuable insights that drive decision-making and business growth.

Custom Logic in Microsoft Dataverse

Microsoft Dataverse offers multiple methods for implementing custom business logic. As a solution architect, it's essential to understand these options to decide which to use based on specific needs. Here's an overview of the primary approaches to implementing custom logic and their limitations.

Types of Custom Logic

1. **Business Rules**

    - No-code logic for simple validations, default values, and visibility rules

    - Limitations: Can only access columns within the table where the rule is applied

2. **Classic Workflows**

    - Automated processes for business logic (e.g., approvals, notifications)

    - Limitations: Can't access rows in one-to-many relationships

3. **Power Automate Cloud Flows**

    - Automates tasks like approvals, data updates, and integrations

    - Asynchronous and flexible but might incur delays if many flows are triggered simultaneously

4. **Business Process Flow**

    - Guides users through predefined stages of a process (e.g., sales process)

    - Used for ensuring consistency and streamlining operations

5. **Calculated Columns**

    - Columns that automatically calculate values based on other fields in the table

    - Limitations: Recalculated only once an hour, and they can't trigger flows

6. **Rollup Columns**

    - Aggregate data from related tables (e.g., summing total sales)

    - Limitations: Recalculated every hour and cannot trigger flows

7. **Plug-ins**

    - Custom logic executed during data transactions, either synchronously or asynchronously

    - Can modify data before or after it's saved to the database

8. **Custom Workflow Assemblies**

    - Extend classic workflows with custom business logic written in code

9. **Custom Actions**

    - Allows creation of reusable processes that can be invoked by other workflows, applications, or APIs

10. **Custom APIs**

    - Allows creating APIs that aggregate operations into a single call, enhancing integration options

11. **Client-Side Scripting**

    - Uses JavaScript or TypeScript for logic that runs in the user's browser, such as form validation or UI changes

12. **Power Apps Component Framework (PCF) Code Components**

    - Custom components that can be added to Power Apps forms, enhancing user interaction

13. **Azure Service Bus and Event Hubs Integration**

    - For high-performance messaging and event-driven architectures, connecting Dataverse with other systems

14. **Webhooks**

    - For notifying external systems of changes within Dataverse

Synchronous vs. Asynchronous Processing

- **Synchronous Processing**

  - The user's screen is blocked while the operation completes. The result is visible immediately.

  - Operations in synchronous calls must complete within two minutes.

  - Examples: Dataverse plug-ins, classic workflows, business rules with Table scope.

- **Asynchronous Processing**

  - The user's screen isn't blocked, and operations are processed in the background, with results shown upon refresh.

  - Includes additional overhead but allows for long-running operations.

  - Examples: Power Automate flows, plug-ins, classic workflows.

Client-Side vs. Server-Side Processing

- **Client-Side Logic**
  - Happens in the app or user interface and provides instant feedback to the user
  - Examples: Canvas app formulas, business rules in Power Apps, Power Apps component framework
- **Server-Side Logic**
  - Happens when data is processed on the server and is visible in the app only after the data is refreshed
  - Examples: Plug-ins, Power Automate flows, classic workflows

Design Considerations

As a solution architect, understanding the constraints and capabilities of each custom logic approach is critical. Consider the following factors:

- **Processing Type (Synchronous vs. Asynchronous):** Choose based on whether immediate feedback or background processing is required.
- **Client vs. Server Logic:** Decide whether the logic needs to run in the user's browser or on the server.
- **Limitations of Each Option:** Each approach has its own set of limitations, such as scope constraints or processing time limits, which must be considered to avoid design bottlenecks.

By understanding and leveraging the different custom logic components available in Microsoft Dataverse, you can create more efficient, scalable, and effective business solutions tailored to your organization's needs.

Platform Limits in Microsoft Power Platform

Microsoft Power Platform imposes several limits on the number of API calls and service resources to ensure efficient performance, maintain stability, and protect against overuse. As a solution architect, it's crucial to understand these limitations and design your solutions in a way that stays within the platform's constraints.

API Requests

API requests encompass actions taken across different products, including Power Apps, Power Automate, and Dataverse. Each API request is counted when a user interacts with the platform in the following ways:

1. **Power Apps**
    - Requests made to connectors and Microsoft Dataverse APIs
2. **Power Automate**
    - All API calls made to connectors, HTTP actions, built-in actions, and even retries from previous failed attempts
3. **Dataverse**
    - Create, read, update, delete (CRUD) operations, assign and share operations, and other system operations (e.g., plug-ins, workflows)

Entitlement Limits

Entitlement limits specify the number of API requests a user is allowed per 24-hour period based on their license. Here's a breakdown of the limits:

- **Paid Licensed Users (Power Platform/Dynamics 365):** 40,000 requests per day
- **Power Apps Pay-As-You-Go Plan:** 6,000 requests per day
- **Power Automate per Flow Plan:** 250,000 requests per day
- **Power Apps Portals (Paid):** 200 requests per day

For **tenant-based API requests**, Microsoft Dataverse allows additional capacity based on subscription type:

- **With at Least One Dynamics 365 Enterprise Subscription:** 100,000 requests per day
- **With at Least One Dynamics 365 Professional Subscription:** 50,000 requests per day
- **With at Least One Microsoft Power Apps or Power Automate Subscription:** 25,000 requests per day

Capacity add-ons are available, raising limits by 10,000 requests per day for each add-on.

Service Limits

Microsoft also imposes **service protection limits** to ensure the stability and quality of service. These limits help to prevent a single user or application from negatively impacting the platform's availability.

Key Service Limits

- **Concurrent Connections:** Limits on the number of connections a user can make to Dataverse at once.

- **API Requests per Connection:** There's a limit to the number of API requests allowed per connection.

- **Runtime Limits per Connection:** Defines how long an API request can run for.

These limits are evaluated within a five-minute sliding window, and exceeding these limits triggers exceptions.

Service protection limits cannot be increased, so your solution must be designed to operate within these constraints.

Retry Policies and Patterns

When a limit is breached, the API responds with a **429 status code** indicating that the limit has been reached. This response includes a Retry-After header specifying the delay before new requests can be processed.

Considerations for Retry Policies

- **Minimize Retries:** Excessive retries can worsen the issue, so your application should back off and retry after the recommended delay.

- **Retry-After Header:** Both the Web API and Organization Service return a Retry-After value indicating how long to wait before retrying.

Minimizing API Calls

To avoid hitting API limits and ensure smooth functionality, you should implement strategies to **minimize the number of API calls**:

1. **Bulk Operations:** When performing data imports or updates, use batch operations to reduce the number of individual API requests.

2. **Efficient Design:** Reduce unnecessary calls by optimizing integrations and workflows.

3. **Strategic Retry:** When retrying failed operations, ensure it is done intelligently to avoid unnecessary load on the platform.

4. **Portal Traffic:** If you have a portal application with anonymous users, watch out for traffic surges that might exceed API limits based on the volume of requests from different users.

5. **Leverage Service Principals:** For applications like portals, service principal accounts can help manage API limits better by grouping requests rather than associating them with individual user accounts.

High Availability Considerations

When designing solutions, **high availability** should be prioritized to ensure that your applications remain functional even under high load. Consider the following:

- **Scalability:** Make sure your architecture can handle increased traffic and API calls without breaching the limits.

- **Retry and Queueing Mechanisms:** Ensure retries are handled appropriately and consider using queues to manage processing tasks asynchronously.

- **Monitoring and Alerts:** Set up monitoring to track API usage and be alerted before limits are reached to take preemptive action.

By carefully designing your solution to optimize API usage, handle retries effectively, and be mindful of service protection limits, you can create applications that remain efficient and scalable while staying within platform limits.

High Availability and Disaster Recovery Considerations for Microsoft Power Platform Solutions

When designing solutions on Microsoft Power Platform, **high availability (HA)** and **disaster recovery (DR)** are crucial aspects that need to be addressed. While Microsoft Power Platform manages the availability and disaster recovery for its core services, the **solution architect** is responsible for ensuring that **non-Microsoft Power Platform components**, **custom code**, and **integrations** are properly designed to withstand outages.

Microsoft Power Platform HA and DR Overview

Microsoft provides built-in high availability and disaster recovery mechanisms for its core services:

1. **Geo-secondary Replicas**

    - For each **production environment** in Power Platform, Microsoft automatically creates **geo-secondary replicas** of the data. These replicas are stored in a secondary region to provide **business continuity** in the event of an **Azure region-wide outage**.

- This means that if one Azure region experiences issues, the data is already replicated to a secondary region and can be recovered quickly, minimizing the impact on services.

2. **Automatic Failover**

   - Microsoft handles failover for Power Platform components. If an issue occurs in the primary **Azure data centers**, the service will automatically failover to a **paired region**. This ensures that users experience minimal service disruption.

   - During failover, users may experience transient errors (e.g., when saving data), but these should resolve quickly without causing significant downtime.

3. **Monitoring**

   - Microsoft continuously monitors the **Power Platform** services as part of its service offering. The platform's built-in monitoring tools and health checks help predict and detect potential issues.

Key Principles for High Availability in Custom Code and Integrations

For non-Microsoft Power Platform components, **custom code**, and **integrations**, architects need to design solutions that account for possible failures and ensure business continuity:

1. **Avoid Single Points of Failure (SPOF)**

    - The solution should be designed with redundancy in mind. Ensure that no single component (e.g., server, database, service) is critical to the operation of the system.

    - Use **load balancing** and **failover mechanisms** to provide continuous availability.

2. **Use Azure Capabilities**

    - Leverage **Azure's built-in high availability features** for custom components, such as **Azure Load Balancer**, **Azure Traffic Manager**, and **Azure Availability Zones** to distribute traffic across multiple instances of your application.

    - For custom code, consider hosting on **Azure App Services** or **Azure Functions**, both of which offer high availability and scaling options.

3. **Monitor and Implement Health Checks**

    - Implement monitoring tools like **Azure Application Insights**, **Azure Monitor**, or custom health check endpoints to detect issues before they affect your users.

    - Regular health checks will help you quickly identify performance bottlenecks or system failures and respond accordingly.

4. **Designing for Transient Failures**

    - Custom integrations with Power Platform or other external services need to be resilient to transient failures. This means your solution should include automatic **retry mechanisms** to handle temporary issues, such as network delays or service unavailability.

- Implement a **back-off strategy** for retries to avoid overwhelming the system with repeated requests during an outage.

5. **Failover Handling for External Integrations**

    - In the event of a failover between paired regions or an Azure region-wide outage, external integrations may face issues. To mitigate this, your solution should leverage **global discovery services** to dynamically detect environment endpoints.

    - Ensure that integrations use **API versioning** and the latest environment endpoints to avoid failures when service endpoints change.

6. **Data Consistency and State Preservation**

    - **Stateful applications** need to preserve the state of their operations across regions or data centers. Consider using **Azure Cosmos DB**, which provides global distribution, or **Azure SQL Database** with geo-replication for high availability and consistency.

    - For data replication, ensure the use of **strong consistency models** and **automatic data synchronization** to avoid discrepancies in the event of failover.

Key Components for Disaster Recovery Strategy

While Microsoft Power Platform provides disaster recovery for its services, custom solutions and integrations should also account for potential failures:

1. **Backup and Restore**

    - For custom databases or external systems integrated with Power Platform, ensure you have robust **backup** and **restore** processes in place to recover from catastrophic failures.

    - Azure Backup and Azure Site Recovery can help automate these processes for custom components.

2. **Disaster Recovery Testing**

    - Regularly test your disaster recovery plan to ensure that the solution can effectively failover to a secondary region, restore services, and maintain business continuity without data loss.

    - Implement **automated testing scripts** to simulate failovers and ensure the recovery mechanisms work as intended.

High Availability Architecture Diagram Example

A typical **high availability architecture** for a solution using Microsoft Power Platform might include

- **Azure Region A (Primary):** Hosting core services, Dataverse, and custom components

- **Azure Region B (Secondary):** Replicating data and services for failover

- **Azure Traffic Manager:** Distributing traffic across regions to ensure availability

- **Power Platform:** With geo-replication and automatic failover to paired regions

- **Custom Integrations:** Leveraging Azure services like Azure Logic Apps or Azure Functions for custom integrations with retries and stateful operations

Exploring Power Apps and Automate

Introduction to Power Apps

As a solution architect, understanding Microsoft Power Apps is crucial when designing and implementing effective business applications. Power Apps allows you to create custom applications with minimal coding effort, enabling rapid development and deployment. In this module, we'll explore the three main types of apps you can build within Power Apps, their capabilities, and how to determine which type best fits your project's needs.

There are three primary types of apps in Power Apps:

1. **Canvas Apps:** These apps provide the most flexibility in terms of design. You have complete control over the layout and appearance of the app. Canvas apps are ideal for scenarios that require customized user interfaces with rich interactivity, such as apps for mobile devices or tablets. You can design apps by dragging and dropping elements onto a canvas and using functions like Microsoft Excel for logic and data management.

CHAPTER 3   GOVERNANCE, ARCHITECTURE, AND CORE COMPONENTS IN POWER PLATFORM AND DYNAMICS 365

2. **Model-Driven Apps:** These apps are built on a data model that you create in Microsoft Dataverse. Instead of designing every screen manually, model-driven apps are built from reusable components like forms, views, and dashboards. This approach is ideal when you need to create applications based on structured data and business processes.

3. **Portal Apps:** Portal apps are external-facing websites that allow secure interactions with external stakeholders. Built on top of Dataverse, these apps expose specific data to users, allowing them to view and update information in a controlled environment.

Microsoft Apps vs. Partner Apps vs. Custom Apps

As a solution architect, one of the first decisions you need to make when designing a solution is whether to use an existing **Microsoft Dynamics 365 app**, a **partner app** from **AppSource**, or to build a **custom app**. Each option comes with its own benefits, and your choice will depend on your specific project requirements.

1. Microsoft Dynamics 365 Apps

Microsoft offers a variety of prebuilt **Dynamics 365 apps**, which are model-driven apps built on top of **Microsoft Dataverse**. These apps are great for standard business processes, such as sales, customer service, and finance. The key here is to evaluate whether the **out-of-the-box** functionality of these apps can meet your needs. If they do, then you can either use them as is or customize them.

2. Partner Apps from AppSource

If the built-in Dynamics 365 apps don't meet your requirements, you can turn to **AppSource**, Microsoft's marketplace for third-party partner apps. These apps can help you extend your solution quickly without starting from scratch. The partner apps on AppSource cover a wide range of functionalities and can easily integrate with Microsoft technologies like **Power Platform** and **Dynamics 365**.

3. Custom Apps

If neither Dynamics 365 apps nor partner apps from AppSource fit your needs, the final option is to create **custom apps** using **Power Apps**. Custom apps allow you to fully tailor the solution to your organization's specific needs, whether it's a **Canvas app**, **model-driven app**, or **portal app**.

Choosing the Right App Type

When choosing which type of app to use, it's important to know the key differences between them:

Model-Driven Apps

- Built on **Dataverse**
- Designed for managing data relationships, with a **consistent UI** and **security trimming**
- Best for business processes and back-office management

Canvas Apps

- Not built on **Dataverse**
- Focuses on a **custom UI** and **device integration**
- Ideal for task-specific, **end user-focused apps**

Portal Apps

- **Dataverse data-driven**
- Designed for **external users**, offering secure access to business data
- Uses web technologies for customization

Common Patterns in App Usage

In many solutions, you will likely use **multiple types of apps**. For example, a **model-driven app** might manage data and processes, while a **Canvas app** could be used for user-focused tasks. **Portal apps** are often employed to provide external users with access to specific data.

Embedding Apps in Teams

Both **Canvas apps** and **model-driven apps** can be added to **Microsoft Teams** for easy access within team channels. Additionally, you can embed **Canvas apps** within a **model-driven app** form to enhance functionality, such as adding visuals or performing complex operations on data.

App Composition

When designing a solution, one of the key decisions you'll make as a solution architect is about **app composition**. This refers to determining the number and type of apps needed for a solution. It involves figuring out how many apps are necessary, what features each app should include, and how to organize them effectively for users.

CHAPTER 3   GOVERNANCE, ARCHITECTURE, AND CORE COMPONENTS IN POWER PLATFORM AND DYNAMICS 365

Deciding on the Number and Type of Apps

Here are some important principles to keep in mind:

- **Avoid large, monolithic apps.** These can become unwieldy and difficult to manage.

- **Don't overwhelm users with too many small apps.** If users have to switch between numerous apps often, it can create a frustrating experience.

- **Reuse components across apps.** By using shared components, you can create different apps for specific user needs without starting from scratch each time.

- **Tailor apps for specific user groups.** For example, offer mobile apps for users who are often away from their desks, ensuring they can stay productive on the go.

It's also essential to consider which **user communities** will use each app, **when** they will use it, and on which devices. Mapping out these factors can help you determine the number and type of apps to create.

Extending Existing Apps vs. Creating New Ones

You have the option to either **extend existing apps** like the **Sales Hub** or **Customer Service Hub** from Dynamics 365 or create **new custom apps**. Here's how to decide:

- **Extending existing apps** may expose you to new features when updates are released but could also include unnecessary features or components that aren't reusable.

- **Creating custom apps** gives you complete control over what's included and allows you to customize the app's forms, views, and navigation as per your requirements.

Choosing the Right Type of App

Now, let's look at the different types of apps:

1. **Model-Driven Apps**

   - Built on top of **Dataverse** and structured around your data model

   - Great for **complex business logic** or managing **business processes** and **data relationships**

   - Provides a consistent UI, making them perfect for tasks where data and processes need to be tracked and managed efficiently

2. **Canvas Apps**

   - More flexible and customizable, Canvas apps let you create a tailored user interface from scratch.

   - They can connect to **multiple data sources** using **connectors** and are ideal for scenarios where a **customized user experience** is key.

   - Best for apps where users need a **graphical, intuitive interface** or tasks like submitting forms on mobile devices.

CHAPTER 3   GOVERNANCE, ARCHITECTURE, AND CORE COMPONENTS IN POWER PLATFORM AND DYNAMICS 365

Components in Power Apps: Enhancing Reusability and Collaboration

As a solution architect, one of the key considerations when building apps in Power Apps is **creating reusable components**. Components promote **efficiency**, **collaboration**, and **consistency** by allowing parts of an app to be reused across multiple apps, making the development process faster and more organized.

Why Are Components Important?

- **Reuse:** Components can be reused within an app and across multiple apps.

- **Collaboration:** Components allow **multiple makers** to work together on the same app, improving teamwork.

- **Consistency and Efficiency:** They help maintain consistent design and functionality, reducing redundancy.

Types of Components in Power Apps

There are two main types of components.

1. Canvas Components

These are targeted at **Canvas app makers** and are **designed for use only in Canvas apps**. They allow app creators to build custom controls that can be reused within a single app or across different Canvas apps. These components help speed up development and ensure consistency.

- **Characteristics of Canvas Components**
  - Ideal for reuse within **Canvas apps**
  - Can be shared across multiple apps
  - Simplify the process for app makers by enabling the reuse of common design elements (e.g., headers, buttons, widgets)
  - Limited to the capabilities of Canvas app formulas and connectors

Canvas components should be stored in **component libraries** for easy reuse, search, and updates. When using component libraries, app makers are notified when there are updates to the components they depend on.

2. Code Components with Power Apps Component Framework

These components are designed for **professional developers**. They offer an enhanced user experience by allowing developers to create custom elements for both **canvas** and **model-driven apps**.

- Characteristics of Code Components
  - Used in **both canvas and model-driven apps** on web and mobile
  - Replace traditional controls like grids and columns
  - Allow for complex customizations and more interactive experiences
  - Require skills in **TypeScript** and **HTML**
  - Can be reused across multiple apps, ensuring performance stays optimal even with multiple components on a form

These components can be **packaged in solutions**, so when an update is made, every app using the component automatically gets the updated version.

Managing Components: Best Practices

- **Component Libraries:** Store and manage canvas components in libraries for easy discovery and updates.

- **Professional Developers:** Use the Power Apps component framework for creating advanced code components that can be used across apps.

- **Strategy for Management:** A solution architect should have a clear strategy for managing components, including deciding when to use canvas components vs. code components, and how to maintain the quality of user experience across apps.

By understanding and implementing these components, solution architects can significantly improve both the efficiency of the app development process and the quality of the user experience across various applications.

Optimizing Canvas Apps: Techniques for Better Performance and User Experience

As a **solution architect**, one of the most critical tasks when developing apps is ensuring that they perform efficiently. While making an app **visually appealing** is essential, it's equally important that the app works smoothly to foster **user adoption.** To achieve this balance, we need to leverage optimization techniques to improve performance and reduce unnecessary complexity.

Understanding Imperative vs. Declarative Development

- **Imperative Development:** This approach focuses on how a task is achieved. It gives developers **more control** but can lead to **complexity** and **more code**.

- **Declarative Development:** This approach focuses on specifying what needs to be done, rather than how. It's simpler, less code-intensive, and more efficient but may offer less control.

Canvas apps often combine **declarative "what"** and optimize the **"how"**. Using **imperative development** for scenarios that can be handled declaratively is often inefficient, leading to performance issues. So as a solution architect, **opt for declarative methods** whenever possible to ensure both simplicity and optimal performance.

Techniques for Optimizing Canvas Apps

1. Offload Work from Apps

Canvas apps may become sluggish when they handle large data sets or execute complex formulas directly within the app. **Offloading work** to other tools or services can help improve performance. For instance:

- Use **Power Automate flows** to offload complex logic.

- Leverage **Dataverse business rules**, **plug-ins**, and **server-side logic** for tasks that don't need to be handled directly in the app.

By **offloading logic**, such as triggering a flow from a Power Apps button to perform data processing or calculations, you reduce the app's workload, making it more responsive.

- **Create Custom Connectors** to Azure Functions or other custom services to offload logic and improve performance.

2. Optimize Data Handling

A common performance issue arises from retrieving large sets of data into collections and then performing client-heavy operations (e.g., JOIN, Sort, Add Column). To mitigate this:

- **Cache Data Locally:** Use the Set function to store data locally, avoiding repeated data retrieval from the source.

- **Use ClearCollect to cache data** locally when the app starts, ensuring that large data operations don't need to be re-executed multiple times.

- **Reduce OnStart formula calls** by minimizing the number of unnecessary data calls triggered when the app launches.

3. Use Concurrent Loading of Data

When loading multiple datasets at once, use the **Concurrent function** to reduce load time. Instead of loading datasets sequentially, which could slow down the app, the **Concurrent function** allows data to be loaded in parallel, improving performance.

- **Without Concurrent**
    - Datasets load one after another, creating delays.

- **With Concurrent**
  - Datasets load simultaneously, reducing overall loading time.

This technique can dramatically improve app startup times.

4. Parallelizing Work

To enhance performance, it's crucial to **parallelize tasks** where possible. For example:

- **Defer tasks** that are not critical and are less likely to be needed immediately.

- Perform **multiple actions simultaneously** using the Concurrent function instead of executing them one after another.

- Monitor app performance continuously to detect bottlenecks and optimize them further.

5. Progress Indicators for Long-Running Tasks

For actions that take a significant amount of time, it's essential to keep the user informed. Display a **progress indicator** to show that the app is processing a task. This helps manage user expectations, improving the overall user experience.

Tools for Monitoring and Testing Canvas Apps

As a solution architect, it's crucial to **test and monitor** Canvas apps to ensure they are performing well. Here are some tools and techniques you can use.

CHAPTER 3   GOVERNANCE, ARCHITECTURE, AND CORE COMPONENTS IN POWER PLATFORM AND DYNAMICS 365

1. Test Studio for Regression Testing

Test Studio allows you to automate tests for your Canvas apps, helping ensure that updates do not break existing functionality. It allows you to

- Organize tests into **test suites**
- Validate app behavior with **test steps** and **assertions**

This helps automate the testing process and ensure consistent app behavior.

2. Azure Monitor and Application Insights

Azure Monitor provides a stream of events that help troubleshoot and diagnose issues in your Canvas app. It helps track app behavior and identify performance issues in real time.

- **Application Insights** (part of Azure Monitor) provides deeper insights into how users are interacting with the app. By connecting your app to Application Insights, you can track
  - Active users
  - Frequent screens
  - User flow across screens
  - Locations where the app is used

This telemetry allows you to understand how your app is used in the real world, which is critical for improving performance and user experience.

3. Monitor Tool for Canvas Apps

Use **Monitor** in Power Apps to trace events during development and runtime. You can track page navigation, screen loads, and user interactions and diagnose any issues quickly.

Canvas App Performance Tuning Strategy

A comprehensive performance-tuning strategy should

1. **Avoid unnecessary work**
2. **Defer tasks** that aren't needed immediately
3. **Parallelize tasks** wherever possible to optimize performance
4. **Monitor app behavior** during runtime to identify and address issues

By constantly evaluating and fine-tuning performance, you can ensure that your Canvas apps not only meet business requirements but also provide an excellent user experience.

As a solution architect, it's crucial to implement these performance optimization techniques, monitor the app's behavior in production, and adapt your strategy based on ongoing insights to maintain optimal performance.

Microsoft Teams and Power Apps: A Seamless Collaboration for Teams

In the modern workplace, **Microsoft Teams** has become the central hub for collaboration, where users spend a significant portion of their day working. To enhance productivity and reduce the need for constant switching between applications, Microsoft allows you to **embed Power Apps directly into Teams**. This enables users to access, interact with, and share data all from within Teams.

CHAPTER 3   GOVERNANCE, ARCHITECTURE, AND CORE COMPONENTS IN POWER
             PLATFORM AND DYNAMICS 365

Creating Power Apps Within Microsoft Teams

Power Apps in Teams allows you to create **Canvas apps** directly within a Teams channel. When you add the **Power Apps application** in Teams, it provides a built-in environment with a **Dataverse for Teams** database. This database acts as a low-code data platform that simplifies the creation of apps within Teams.

Here's how it works:

- **Dataverse for Teams** is a built-in data platform designed specifically for Teams, offering **relational data storage**, rich data types, and enterprise-grade governance.

- **Power Apps Studio**, embedded within the Power Apps app in Teams, enables app makers to create, edit, and share apps within the team, all without leaving the Teams environment.

- You can quickly create **Teams-specific apps** tied to custom data tables that meet your team's unique needs.

This integrated experience simplifies app creation for Teams users. If you already have **Microsoft 365 access**, you don't need any additional licenses to use the app or data. The advantage here is that it significantly reduces friction for app makers and users alike.

Advantages of Using Dataverse for Teams

- **Relational Data Storage:** Easily store and manage data within Teams.

- **Rich Data Types:** Leverage various data types for creating dynamic apps.

- **Simple Deployment:** Deploy apps directly to the Teams app store with a single click.

- **No Extra Licensing:** If you're a Microsoft 365 user, you can start building and using apps without needing additional licenses.

Limitations of Dataverse for Teams

While Dataverse for Teams is a powerful tool for building lightweight apps directly within Teams, there are a few important **limitations** to consider, particularly when designing solutions for larger or more complex scenarios:

1. **No API Access:** You don't have access to APIs to connect with external systems or databases. This can limit integration options.

2. **Limited Control Support:** Some advanced app controls, typically available in full Dataverse, may not be supported in Dataverse for Teams.

3. **Canvas Apps Only:** Only Canvas apps can be created and used within Dataverse for Teams. Model-driven apps or other advanced app types are not supported.

4. **No AI Builder Support:** The use of AI Builder, which is available in the full Dataverse, is not supported in Dataverse for Teams. This means you can't integrate AI capabilities like text recognition or form processing into your apps.

CHAPTER 3   GOVERNANCE, ARCHITECTURE, AND CORE COMPONENTS IN POWER PLATFORM AND DYNAMICS 365

As a **solution architect**, when considering **Dataverse for Teams** for app creation within a **Microsoft Teams** environment, it's essential to keep these limitations in mind. While the platform is well-suited for simple, lightweight solutions directly within Teams, it may not be appropriate for apps requiring advanced features like complex integrations, AI capabilities, or extensive custom controls.

As part of your role as a solution architect, you need to **evaluate the specific needs of your team or organization:**

- For **small-scale, team-specific apps** that don't require extensive external integrations or advanced functionality, Dataverse for Teams is an excellent, cost-effective choice.

- For **larger, more complex solutions**, or scenarios where API access or AI features are needed, you may need to look at other solutions that provide the full capabilities of **Dataverse**.

By understanding both the strengths and limitations of Dataverse for Teams, you can make informed decisions that meet the needs of your users without compromising on functionality or performance.

Power Apps Portals: Exposing Dataverse Data to Internal and External Audiences

Power Apps portals are designed to provide an easy way to display and interact with Microsoft Dataverse data on an externally facing website. This is a powerful tool for allowing both internal and external users to access and update data securely.

Key Features of Power Apps Portals

Power Apps portals are built on top of **Microsoft Dataverse**, which means they benefit from all the features of model-driven apps. Here are some of the key features of Power Apps portals:

- **Centralized Management:** Manage and configure your portal from a centralized location.

- **Common Data Model (CDM):** Leverage the standardized structure of the data model to ensure consistency across systems.

- **Roles and Permissions:** Define user roles and set permissions to control access to the portal data.

- **Forms and Views:** Create and manage forms and views that display Dataverse data in a structured and user-friendly way.

- **Business Rules:** Use business rules to implement logic and validate data within the portal.

- **Declarative Workflows and Actions:** Automate processes without writing code, using built-in workflows and actions.

- **Plug-in Architecture:** Extend functionality by integrating with custom plug-ins.

- **Integration with Other Services:** Easily integrate with external services and applications.

- **Dataverse Extensibility:** Customize the portal's behavior using Dataverse's extensibility features.

- **Audit:** Track changes and access to ensure data security and governance.

The content in Power Apps portals is stored directly in **Dataverse**, making it easy to edit and manage content using both the **Power Apps Portals Studio** and the **Portal Management app**. Additionally, Dataverse's robust security model ensures that only authorized users can access sensitive data.

Portal Architecture

Power Apps portals interact directly with Dataverse, allowing users to access and manage data through **forms** and **views**. The portals provide built-in components that use model-driven views and forms, but they can also be customized and extended based on specific needs.

Portal architecture ensures that portals can securely extend Dataverse solutions to both internal and external audiences. Users can access portals in two ways:

- **Anonymous Users**: No authentication required.

- **Authenticated Users**: Users must log in via supported identity providers like **Microsoft Azure B2C**, **Microsoft Entra ID**, or other external identity providers.

When to Use Power Apps Portals

Power Apps portals are ideal for specific use cases, such as

- **Secure Interactions with Dataverse:** When you need secure access to Dataverse data for both internal and external users.

- **Community or Self-Service Sites:** Build sites for customer service, employee self-service, or partner portals.

- **CRUD Operations on Dataverse Data:** Allow users to create, read, update, and delete (CRUD) records in Dataverse.

- **Business-User Friendly:** If you have limited resources or budget and prefer no-code configurations.

- **Multi-device and Responsive:** Portals are designed to be responsive, ensuring users can access them across all devices and browsers.

- **Multilingual Support:** Power Apps portals support multilingual implementations, making it ideal for global audiences.

- **Single Sign-On (SSO):** Seamlessly authenticate users with SSO.

When to Exercise Caution

While Power Apps portals are powerful, they may not be suitable for all scenarios. Consider the following before implementing:

- **External Data:** If most of your data is stored outside of Dataverse (e.g., in another external system), Power Apps portals may not be the best fit.

- **Heavy Document Management:** Portals are not ideal for environments requiring extensive document management, indexing, and searching.

- **Large Volumes of Users:** If you expect heavy traffic or large volumes of users accessing the portal, performance might become an issue.

- **E-Commerce Needs:** If your portal involves e-commerce functionality like processing payments or maintaining an online store, Power Apps portals may not be the right tool.

- **Direct Power Apps User Access:** For certain use cases, it might be more appropriate to provide direct Power Apps access to licensed users rather than using a portal.

Authentication Considerations

Power Apps portals support both **authenticated** and **unauthenticated** user access. As a solution architect, you need to consider how users will authenticate:

- **Microsoft Azure B2C** or **Microsoft Entra ID** can be used to authenticate external users.

- Avoid using **locally stored accounts** for authentication, as it can lead to security issues.

Implementation Considerations

When implementing a portal app, keep these factors in mind:

- **Template Choice:** Decide whether to start with a blank portal template or use a pre-configured **Dynamics 365 template** (e.g., for customer self-service or employee portals).

- **Custom Templates:** Understand the gaps between the provided templates and your specific requirements and be prepared to customize the portal.

- **Liquid Template Skills:** Some portal pages may require advanced customization using **Liquid templates**. Make sure your team has the skills needed.

- **User Data Access:** Identify what data authenticated users will need to access and ensure proper permissions and security controls are in place.

Deployment Considerations

- **Portal Configuration:** Portal configurations (such as views and forms) can be packaged within solutions, but most of the portal configurations are stored in Dataverse tables. Tools like the **Configuration Migration tool** can assist in moving portal configurations from **development to test to production** environments.

Automation Options for Solution Architects in Power Automate

As a solution architect, it's essential to understand the various automation options available in **Microsoft Power Automate** when designing a solution. The ability to choose the right tool for automating business processes can significantly impact efficiency and scalability. This module helps you evaluate the different automation options and make informed decisions based on the business needs.

Key Automation and Custom Logic Options

There are several automation options available within **Microsoft Dataverse**, each suited to different use cases:

1. Business rules
2. Classic workflows
3. Plug-ins

4. Power Automate Cloud Flows

5. Power Automate Desktop Flows

Let's dive deeper into each option and explore when it's best to use them.

1. Business Rules

Business rules are lightweight, no-code logic tools that help enforce simple validations and data transformations in **model-driven apps** or at the **data layer**.

- **Purpose:** Business rules are used to validate data or set values automatically within the system.

- **Characteristics**

  - Best for simple logic such as showing/hiding fields or setting field values

  - Operate on a **single record** within a model-driven app and can be triggered during data transactions

  - **Limited Scope:** Can't access related records or external data

  - **No Connectors:** Cannot integrate with other services

When to use: Business rules are ideal for simple validations, such as ensuring required fields are filled or calculations are made when a record is being updated. They're optimized for easy, no-code configuration.

2. Classic Workflows

Classic workflows in Dataverse are designed to automate business processes by performing tasks that would typically require manual intervention.

- **Purpose:** Classic workflows help automate processes like sending emails, creating records, or updating related records.

- **Characteristics**
  - Suitable for **real-time** processing
  - Can handle **related records** in many-to-one relationships
  - Limited to operations within **Dataverse** data

When to use: Classic workflows are useful for automating tasks that need to occur immediately after an event (like updating a record upon submission of a form). However, **Power Automate** should generally be the first choice for most background automation needs.

3. Plug-ins

A **plug-in** is a custom .NET assembly that can be uploaded to Microsoft Dataverse and used to respond to events or modify default platform behavior.

- **Purpose:** Plug-ins allow for complex, custom logic that can execute during specific events (e.g., when a record is created or updated).

- **Characteristics**

  - Requires development skills to write custom code

  - Can run synchronously or asynchronously

  - Best for handling **complex logic** or modifying the **request/response** behavior instantly

When to use: Plug-ins are perfect for complex business logic that goes beyond what can be accomplished with no-code options like business rules or workflows. They offer the flexibility to extend Dataverse operations with highly customized logic.

4. Power Automate Cloud Flows

Power Automate Cloud Flows are workflows that allow you to automate repetitive tasks and streamline business processes within and across various systems.

- **Purpose:** Automate processes that span multiple systems, including sending notifications, handling approvals, or gathering data

- **Characteristics**

  - Best for **non-real-time automation** (though they can be near real time depending on triggers)

  - Can integrate with hundreds of cloud-based services and APIs using **connectors**

  - Great for orchestrating workflows across multiple systems, like sending an approval request via email after a record is updated in Dataverse

CHAPTER 3   GOVERNANCE, ARCHITECTURE, AND CORE COMPONENTS IN POWER PLATFORM AND DYNAMICS 365

When to use: Cloud flows are the go-to tool for automating processes that don't need to be processed immediately but require coordination across different systems, such as integrating data from a third-party system into Dataverse.

5. Power Automate Desktop Flows

Power Automate Desktop Flows use **Robotic Process Automation (RPA)** to automate tasks on desktop applications and web interfaces, particularly those that don't have APIs or connectors.

- **Purpose:** Automate tasks on desktop or web applications that don't have built-in integrations

- **Characteristics**

    - **Attended:** Require a user to manually trigger the automation

    - **Unattended:** Can be run on virtual machines without user interaction

    - Ideal for automating tasks in **legacy applications** that lack APIs

When to use: Desktop flows are best for automating processes in legacy systems where APIs or connectors don't exist, or for tasks that involve manual data entry into applications.

6. Connectors for Dataverse

Power Automate offers several connectors to interact with Dataverse data:

- **Microsoft Dataverse Connector:** This is the most recommended connector for Dataverse, providing flexibility and a wide range of available triggers and actions.

- **Dynamics 365 Connectors:** These are used for specialized Dataverse data, such as Dynamics 365 Sales Insights or Dynamics 365 Business Central.

- **Legacy Dataverse Connector:** Deprecated and should only be used for compatibility with older solutions.

Assessing the Cost of Automation

When deciding on an automation strategy, it's important to balance the **business value** of automation with the **cost** of doing so. A solution architect should consider

- **Development Time:** How long will it take to build and deploy the solution?

- **License Costs:** Consider the ongoing costs for Power Automate licenses.

- **Business Value:** What benefit will the automation provide? Will it streamline operations or reduce manual work?

- **Cost of Doing Nothing:** What's the cost of continuing with the current manual process? This could include inefficiency, delays, or potential errors.

Triggers in Power Automate

In Power Automate, a **trigger** is an event that initiates a cloud flow. Triggers can be set off by user actions, scheduled events, or connector-generated events, such as new records being added or modified. The triggers available in Power Automate depend on the connector being used.

Types of Connectors

There are two primary types of connectors used in Power Automate:

1. **Tabular Connectors:** These connectors are used for data sources that store data in tables. For example, Dataverse is a tabular connector and supports triggers such as the creation, update, or deletion of records.

2. **Function-Based Connectors:** These connectors are related to cloud services like Twitter or Outlook. For example, an Outlook trigger might activate when an email is received.

Trigger Types

Power Automate supports three main types of triggers to initiate cloud flows:

1. **Automated Trigger:** These flows are triggered automatically by specific events, such as when a new record is created or when a file appears in a designated folder.

2. **Instant Trigger:** These flows are initiated by a user, such as selecting a button in an app to start a process.

3. **Scheduled Trigger:** These flows run on a set schedule, like every day at 9:00 AM, or every hour.

For example, with the Dataverse connector, an automated flow can be triggered when a record is added, modified, or deleted. The trigger condition can be set to different variations, such as

- Added
- Added or deleted
- Added or modified
- Added, modified, or deleted
- Modified
- Modified or deleted

Additionally, Dataverse connectors support **instant triggers**, such as when a row is selected in a model-driven app form or a business process flow step. This allows users to manually start a flow.

Poll vs. Push Triggers

Triggers in Power Automate fall into two categories:

1. **Polling Triggers:** These triggers repeatedly check the API at specified intervals to see if new data is available. When new data is found, the flow is triggered. An example would be a timer-based trigger.

2. **Push Triggers:** These are more efficient and activate in real time when new data is pushed from a service, such as the Dataverse connector.

Push triggers are the preferred method since they reduce unnecessary checks and provide a more immediate response.

If a connector does not have a trigger, you can still use a **scheduled trigger** to check for data changes from the previous run, essentially using a polling pattern.

Using Filters

To optimize the efficiency of your cloud flows, solution architects should minimize unnecessary flow runs. A common mistake is to retrieve data in the trigger and then check if the flow should continue, which wastes resources. With Dataverse connectors, the trigger already includes the new or modified data, so no need to retrieve it again.

You can apply **filters** to your triggers to limit the data the flow will process. These filters include

1. **Select Columns:** You can specify the columns that should be considered when a change happens. The flow will trigger only if there's a change in one of these columns.

2. **Row Filter:** You can apply an OData expression to filter rows. This limits the flow to consider only rows that meet certain conditions, improving performance.

Ensuring Only Changed Data Is Processed

While filters can limit which rows trigger a flow, it's important to note that simply including a column in the trigger's output doesn't guarantee the value of that column has changed. If you need to ensure that only updated values are processed, you may need to use a **plug-in with Pre- and Post-Images** to track changes accurately.

In summary, when working with Power Automate triggers, it's crucial to select the appropriate type of trigger, use filters to minimize unnecessary flow runs, and be mindful of the data changes that actually need to be processed.

Common Actions in Power Automate (with Dataverse Connector)

In Power Automate, **actions** are tasks that occur after a flow is triggered. The actions you can use depend on the connector being utilized. For Dataverse, there are various actions available that allow you to manage data and files and perform business processes.

Key Dataverse Actions

Here are some of the most common actions available with the Dataverse connector:

1. **Add a New Row:** This action allows you to add a new record to the selected environment.

2. **Delete a Row:** Deletes a specific record from a selected environment.

3. **Download a File or an Image:** Used to download files or images stored in Dataverse.

4. **Get a Row by ID:** Retrieves a record by its unique ID from Dataverse.

5. **List Rows:** Retrieves a list of records from Dataverse. You can apply filters using OData or FetchXML queries to customize the data retrieved.

6. **Perform a Background Operation:** This action is used for long-running operations and is currently in preview.

7. **Perform a Bound Action:** Executes actions associated with a specific table in Dataverse.

8. **Perform an Unbound Action:** Executes actions that are not associated with a particular table but are set globally.

9. **Relate and Unrelate Rows:** These actions allow you to create or remove relationships between records in Dataverse.

10. **Update a Row:** Updates an existing record. It's efficient to only include the fields that have changed to avoid unnecessary updates.

Retrieving Data

When using actions like **Get a row by ID** or **List rows** to retrieve data, it's crucial to focus on retrieving only the fields you need, as Dataverse includes a lot of metadata by default.

- **Get a Row by ID**: This action retrieves a single record, but it does not include related lookup fields, so if these are required, a separate action might be necessary.

- **List Rows**: This action can retrieve multiple records, and you can apply filters directly in the **List rows** action. It is more efficient to filter data here rather than in subsequent steps using data operations.

You can also use **OData queries** or **FetchXML queries** to refine your data retrieval. Dataverse also supports pagination if your query returns more than 1024 rows (up to a maximum of 100,000 rows).

Updating Data

When using the **Update a row** action:

- **Only include changed columns** to avoid unnecessary operations. This approach minimizes the risk of triggering other automation or audit logging and also a row required where condition to update a specific row.

- You can use the **null expression** to clear values in fields that need to be reset.

- Make sure to provide the **GUID (Global Unique Identifier)** for the primary key. If you're using an alternate key, the system will perform an **upsert** operation (update or insert).

Calling Custom Actions

In Dataverse, custom actions are reusable processes that you can trigger both from within Power Automate and external code. These actions are similar to workflows and can involve conditions and record manipulation.

- **Perform a Bound Action:** Use this for actions associated with a specific Dataverse table (entity).

- **Perform an Unbound Action:** Use this for actions that are global in nature and not tied to a specific table.

Some built-in actions include

- **Set Word Template:** Creates a Word document based on a predefined template

- **Add to Queue:** Adds a record to a queue for processing

Error Handling in Power Automate

When building flows in Power Automate, handling errors gracefully is crucial to ensure that your flows are reliable and don't disrupt business processes. As a solution architect, it's important to plan how errors should be handled within your flows, especially in mission-critical applications.

Run After Settings

The **Run After** feature in Power Automate allows you to define how a subsequent step should behave based on the outcome of previous steps. The available settings for controlling how a flow behaves after an action completes are

1. **Is Successful (default):** The action runs if the previous action completed successfully.

2. **Has Timed Out:** The action runs if the previous action has timed out.

3. **Is Skipped:** The action runs if the previous action was skipped.

4. **Has Failed:** The action runs if the previous action failed.

You can customize the **Run After** settings by clicking on the **Settings** tab of a step, where you'll find an option to specify the conditions under which the current step will execute. For example, you can configure an action like "Send a push notification" to run only if a previous step, such as "Get a row by ID," fails. This way, you can notify someone if an error occurs.

Additionally, each action in Power Automate has a color-coding system that provides a visual cue about the action's behavior. For instance, when you set an action to "Has failed," a red dot appears, signaling that the flow is set to react to failure.

Parallel Branches and Error Handling

If you want to handle success and failure scenarios separately, you can use **parallel branches**. Parallel branches allow you to configure different actions to take place based on the success or failure of a previous step. For example, one branch might handle the scenario when a step is successful, while the other branch can handle failure cases. This helps ensure that you manage multiple scenarios in the flow without needing to manually control every possible outcome.

Changesets for Data Integrity

When performing multiple actions on Dataverse data, it's essential to maintain **data integrity**. The **Perform a changeset request** action allows you to group several operations (like Create, Update, and Delete) into a single transaction. If any of the actions fail, the entire changeset is rolled back, ensuring that the data remains consistent, and no partial changes are committed.

However, keep in mind that changesets are only available with **Create**, **Update**, and **Delete** actions in the Dataverse connector, and they can only be used in the **classic designer**.

Handling API Limits

Power Automate enforces **API limits** to protect the platform from excessive load. Some important limits to consider when building your flows include

- **Loop Limits:** The **Apply to each** loop can only process up to **100,000 iterations**. If your flow involves processing large data sets, you might need to partition the work into smaller batches.

- **Do Until Loop:** The **Do Until** loop runs up to 60 iterations or 1 hour by default. You can modify these settings, but if you exceed the limits, the flow will exit without an error.

- **Flow Duration:** A flow can run for a maximum of 30 days. If your flow involves long-running processes, it's better to use **scheduled flows** to periodically check if a row needs to be processed.

- **API Throttling:** Connectors like the **Dataverse connector** have throttling limits. For example, the Dataverse connector allows only **6,000 API calls** per connection every 300 seconds. Be mindful of these limits to avoid flow interruptions.

Business Process Flows in Power Automate and Power Platform

In the Power Platform, **business process flows (BPFs)** are a powerful tool that helps guide users through structured, multistep processes within **model-driven apps**. They ensure that business processes are followed consistently and help users understand where they are in the process and what data is required to complete the next stage.

Structure of Business Process Flows

A **Business Process Flow** consists of two main components:

1. **Stages:** These represent major phases in the process. Each stage is linked to a **Dataverse table**.

2. **Steps:** Each step corresponds to fields (columns) in the table, and they define the required actions or information for that stage.

The flow appears as an interactive guide at the top of the form within a model-driven app, allowing users to track their progress and move through the necessary steps to complete the process.

Key Features of Business Process Flows

- **Stage Gating:** You can set specific steps within a stage as **mandatory**, so the user cannot move to the next stage until those steps are completed. This ensures that no important steps are skipped.

- **Conditional Branching:** Business process flows can adapt based on the values entered in previous steps. For example, depending on the data provided in one stage, the next stage may change or take a different path.

- **Multiple Tables:** A business process flow can include up to **five tables** in the flow, enabling it to work across multiple entities in Dataverse, providing a more comprehensive process management approach.

- **Switching Between Processes:** Users can switch from one business process flow to another at any time. This flexibility helps when a user's needs change during the flow execution.

- **Security Integration:** Business process flows can be **security-bound**, meaning different users or groups can be assigned different business process flows based on their roles, ensuring tailored experiences for different users.

Process Table and Reporting

When a business process flow is created, a **process table** is automatically generated. This table tracks the **instances** of the business process flow and its current stage. The process table can be added to model-driven app navigation, and you can generate **reports**, **charts**, and **dashboards** to visualize the progress and usage of the flow.

There's also a **Power BI template app** available for visualizing and analyzing the progress of business process flows across your organization.

Automation and API Integration

Business process flows can be automated using Power Automate or developer APIs. You can configure Power Automate to **start** or **stop** a business process flow automatically based on triggers or conditions, enhancing workflow automation.

Using the API, developers can control the business process flow at a programmatic level, enabling custom business rules or advanced automation scenarios.

Use Cases for Business Process Flows

Business process flows are ideal for scenarios such as

- **Outcome-Oriented Processes:** Business process flows are not just for data capture—they help guide users toward achieving specific outcomes.

- **Linking Related Tables:** A BPF can automatically switch between related tables as the process progresses. This action hides the complexity of the underlying data model from the user.

- **Triggering Automation:** Automation can be triggered based on progress through different stages of the business process. For example, when a process moves from the "Review" stage to the "Approval" stage, an approval email might be sent out automatically.

Branching vs. Multiple Processes

When designing a business process flow, you may need to decide whether to

- **Use One Process with Multiple Branches:** This allows you to have different paths within a single process based on conditions or user inputs.

- **Create Multiple Processes:** This approach might be more appropriate if the processes are very different from one another.

To make this decision, consider the following questions:

- Do the processes need to run **concurrently**?

- Does the process need to **return to the same place** after branching?

- How will you **determine which process is applied** to new records?

Immersive Business Process Flows

In addition to being used within model-driven apps, business process flows can also be utilized **standalone**. These are referred to as **immersive business process flows** and are often used with a **per-process license**.

To create an immersive business process flow, simply choose **None** for the table to associate the flow with. This allows the flow to be used independently, where it can still have its own process table, and you can add columns, create forms, and store data within the table.

Conclusion

Governance, architecture, app development, and automation are the cornerstones of successful Power Platform and Dynamics 365 projects. By mastering these areas, you can ensure projects are well-structured, solutions are scalable and secure, and business processes are seamlessly automated. As you move forward, apply these principles to create innovative solutions, streamline workflows, and deliver transformative value. With the Power Platform, the journey from concept to impactful solutions has never been more accessible.

CHAPTER 4

Leveraging Microsoft Copilot and RPA and Securing Data Models in Power Platform Solutions

Chapter Goal: To help readers understand how to leverage Microsoft Copilot and Robotic Process Automation (RPA) to enhance business efficiency, and to provide comprehensive guidance on building secure and effective data models for Power Platform solutions. By the end of this chapter, readers will be able to integrate AI-driven assistance and automation into their workflows while ensuring robust data architecture and security.

CHAPTER 4 LEVERAGING MICROSOFT COPILOT AND RPA AND SECURING DATA MODELS IN POWER PLATFORM SOLUTIONS

Sub-topics:

1. Exploring Microsoft Copilot and Robotic Process Automation

2. Data Modeling and Security for Power Platform Solutions

Introduction

In today's rapidly evolving digital landscape, AI-powered tools and automation are redefining how businesses operate. Microsoft Copilot brings AI-driven assistance to various Microsoft applications, enabling users to achieve more with intelligent suggestions and automation. Coupled with Robotic Process Automation (RPA), organizations can streamline repetitive tasks, improve accuracy, and optimize resource allocation.

Equally important is the ability to design secure and efficient data models for Power Platform solutions. Strong data modeling ensures the foundation for apps and workflows is scalable and aligns with business needs, while security measures safeguard sensitive information and ensure compliance with regulations.

In this chapter, we'll dive into how Microsoft Copilot enhances user productivity, explore RPA's potential in automating business processes, and provide a detailed guide to effective data modeling and security practices. Together, these elements form a powerful toolkit for creating intelligent, secure, and efficient Power Platform solutions.

CHAPTER 4   LEVERAGING MICROSOFT COPILOT AND RPA AND SECURING DATA MODELS IN POWER PLATFORM SOLUTIONS

Robotic Process Automation (RPA) Overview

We're diving into **Robotic Process Automation (RPA)** and its role in automating tasks, specifically using **Microsoft Power Automate for desktop flows**.

Many older software applications don't have modern APIs for accessing their data or functions, making them tricky to automate directly. Here's where RPA comes in—it works by capturing the steps a user performs in an application's interface and then repeating those steps to automate tasks. Essentially, RPA mimics a user's actions within an app to carry out automated tasks.

RPA is a game-changer. By automating repetitive and simple tasks, it can lower operational costs, reduce human error, and free up time for more valuable activities.

Challenges with Legacy Systems

Many organizations rely on **legacy systems**—older software that lacks the modern APIs required for smooth automation. These systems often operate on premises, making them tough to integrate into cloud-based workflows.

Moreover, replacing legacy systems can be difficult and costly. This is where **Power Automate for desktop flows** provides a solution. It allows you to automate processes even in applications that don't have API access.

The Power of Automation with Power Automate

While some cloud-based services come with modern APIs, there are still plenty of cases where these aren't available. Power Automate helps overcome this by offering tools that can integrate with applications that don't have APIs.

CHAPTER 4   LEVERAGING MICROSOFT COPILOT AND RPA AND SECURING DATA MODELS IN POWER PLATFORM SOLUTIONS

Microsoft's approach to automation can be broken down into key goals:

- **Accelerating Productivity:** By eliminating time-consuming manual tasks, employees can focus more on strategic work.

- **Scaling Automation:** Whether you're a user, developer, or IT professional, Power Automate lets everyone automate workflows for both on-premises and cloud apps.

- **Intelligent Automation:** By combining AI with automation, tasks become even more streamlined and efficient.

- **Secure Integration:** Power Automate enables users to build workflows that follow security policies, freeing up IT teams for more complex tasks.

A good starting point for automation is understanding the workflows that need improvement and identifying the right solutions for automation.

Role of a Solution Architect

As a **solution architect**, your role is to design automated workflows that integrate both **cloud-based services** and **legacy applications** (whether desktop or web). Here's how to spot great opportunities for automation:

- **Standard Processes:** If the process is consistent and well-understood, it's a strong candidate for automation.

- **High Frequency:** Processes that are frequently repeated have a higher return on investment (ROI) when automated.

- **Predictability:** If the process is predictable and doesn't require complex judgment calls, it's ideal for automation.

- **Prone to Human Error:** If a process is error-prone due to manual input, automation can help mitigate mistakes.

- **High Risk and Impact:** For processes where failure could lead to significant consequences, automation can reduce the risk and impact of errors.

Desktop flows are a great fit for scenarios involving repetitive tasks like form processing, data extraction, or claim handling. They're particularly useful when you have rule-based processes that can be easily automated.

Even when an API is available, it might not expose all functions available in the app's UI. In such cases, Power Automate for desktop can provide the solution.

Best Practices for Designing Flows

When designing automation, it's better to break down large, complex processes into smaller flows. Here's why:

- **Collaboration:** Smaller flows allow multiple people to work on the same project.

- **Reusability:** Small, common steps can be reused across different processes.

- **Simpler Error Handling:** With smaller flows, managing errors becomes much easier.

- **Easier Maintenance:** Updating smaller flows is more straightforward, and failures are easier to manage.

In summary, RPA is a powerful tool for automating tasks that don't have easy access to modern APIs. By leveraging Power Automate, you can streamline processes, reduce errors, and increase efficiency, making it an essential part of any solution architect's toolkit.

Power Automate for Desktop

When it comes to automating tasks with **legacy applications** that don't have available APIs or connectors, **Power Automate for desktop** is your go-to solution. These desktop flows use **Robotic Process Automation (RPA)** techniques, simulating user actions on an application's interface to carry out tasks.

How It Works

Power Automate for desktop flows operate by **recording user actions**—things like mouse clicks, keyboard inputs, and data entry. It also extracts data from the user interface (UI) of legacy apps. Once these actions are recorded, the **Power Automate for desktop editor** allows you to fine-tune and adjust them to create more complex automation processes.

Whether you're working with modern cloud-based applications or older on-premises legacy systems, Power Automate for desktop can automate **rule-based UI tasks**. And you have the flexibility to run these flows in two ways:

- **Attended:** The user manually triggers the flow.
- **Unattended:** The flow runs on a **Microsoft Azure Virtual Machine**, without user intervention.

This is particularly useful when there's no other way to integrate an application, or doing so would be too costly and time-consuming.

Desktop Software Requirements

Unlike the cloud-based components of the Power Platform, **Power Automate for desktop** requires installation on your local machine. Here's what you need:

- **Supported OS:** Windows 10/11, Windows Server 2016, or 2019. For **unattended flows**, **Windows 11 Home** won't work—you'll need **Windows 11 Pro or Enterprise**.

- **Installation:** You can download the **Power Automate for desktop setup** from the Power Automate portal. Don't forget to check the option to install the **machine-runtime app**, which connects your local device to the cloud portal.

Deployment and IT Coordination

As a **solution architect**, you'll need to coordinate with your **IT department** to plan the installation and licensing of **Power Automate Desktop (PAD)**. It's essential to handle this early in the process because local software installations can sometimes take longer than expected due to IT policies.

For larger-scale deployments, **silent installations** (mass deployment) are supported through a service principal account. Your IT team can handle these installations remotely. Also, note that **Power Automate for Desktop** requires **Premium Licensing** for connecting to the cloud portal.

Browser Requirements

To interact with **web applications**, you'll need a **modern web browser**. Supported browsers include

- Google Chrome
- Microsoft Edge
- Mozilla Firefox

When you install the latest version of Power Automate for desktop, these browser extensions are included automatically. If you're using an older version (2.27 or earlier), you'll need to install the browser extension separately, and your IT team may need to configure it due to corporate restrictions.

Integration with Microsoft Power Platform

Power Automate for desktop integrates with **Microsoft Power Platform**, leveraging **Microsoft Dataverse**. For this, you'll need a **Microsoft Power Platform environment** with Dataverse support, and if one doesn't exist, you'll need to create a database for the default environment. You'll also need **Premium Licensing** for full interaction with the cloud portal.

Solutions and Application Lifecycle Management (ALM)

Desktop flows are **solution-aware**, meaning they can be included in a solution and managed throughout the application lifecycle management. To ensure portability and smooth deployment across environments, it's a best practice to use **environment variables** for any properties in the desktop flow that might change between environments.

Deployment Steps

Once your desktop flow is ready and deployed, there are a few manual steps to complete:

- **Power Automate Machine Runtime:** Ensure your device connects to the appropriate environment.

- **Set Environment Variables:** Adjust them according to the specific environment.

- **User Authentication:** Configure authentication so that the flow can perform actions on the user's behalf.

As the solution architect, it's your job to ensure these deployment steps are clearly defined and included in the solution deployment plan.

In summary, **Power Automate for desktop** is an invaluable tool for automating tasks in legacy applications or when there's no API available. By working closely with IT to manage the installation, deployment, and licensing, you can create effective automation solutions that save time and reduce errors across both modern and legacy systems.

Record and Edit Tasks in Power Automate for Desktop

Power Automate for desktop offers powerful functionality to **record** tasks and **edit** the steps in desktop flows, which is essential for automating repetitive actions on applications. This can significantly streamline processes, especially when working with legacy systems or applications without connectors.

Recording Tasks

When using Power Automate for desktop, there are two primary ways to record tasks:

1. **Record:** The basic **recording** feature captures actions performed in both **Windows native applications** and **web applications**. It identifies and highlights elements like buttons, menus, and fields in the application's UI. When you click on these elements or type into fields, it records the mouse and keyboard actions associated with them. If an incorrect action is captured, you can easily **delete it**. The **Reset** option allows you to start over if necessary.

2. **Record with Copilot (Preview):** This feature leverages **AI** to enhance the recording process by capturing **voice**, **screens**, and **mouse movements**. You can simply describe what you want Copilot to do, and it will record the task for you. Once the recording is complete, you can review and edit the steps as needed. This feature is in preview, but it adds a level of automation and ease to the task recording process.

Editing Steps and Actions

Once the tasks are recorded, you can fine-tune them by **editing the steps**. For example, you might need to **remove unnecessary actions** or **add new actions** to enhance the flow. You can also modify the objects that were selected in the application and add **new UI elements** to the recorded actions.

Power Automate for desktop offers many capabilities to interact with systems and perform actions, such as

- Running **SQL queries** against a database
- Manipulating data in **Microsoft Excel**
- Processing emails in **Microsoft Outlook**
- Running **PowerShell scripts**
- Copying data to/from the **clipboard**
- Accessing **Azure AD** objects and **cloud services**

As a **solution architect**, it's important to choose the right technology for each task. For example, if you need to execute a SQL query, you should decide whether to use a desktop flow, a cloud flow, or an **Azure function**, depending on the context.

Variables in Desktop Flows

Variables are an essential part of Power Automate for desktop. They allow information to change during each run of a desktop flow. If you're automating data entry, **flow variables** help define the fields to be filled. Here's a breakdown of how variables work:

- **Input Variables:** These are the pieces of information that you pass into a desktop flow to drive the process.
- **Output Variables:** These are the results or outcomes that the desktop flow returns after execution.

One of the key features of Power Automate for desktop is the ability to **integrate with cloud flows.** You can pass **input variables** from a cloud flow and return **output variables** back to the cloud flow. This integration allows for seamless automation across both desktop and cloud environments.

To manage environments, if input variables vary between different environments, **environment variables** should be defined. This ensures the flow adapts as it moves between different contexts.

As a **solution architect**, it's crucial to encourage the use of variables and ensure a **naming convention** is in place to maintain clarity and organization, especially when working across different flows and environments. Make sure to define input and output variables at the design stage, as cloud and desktop flows may be built by different teams or makers.

Running Desktop Flows

In Power Automate for desktop, you can run desktop flows in two main modes: **Attended** and **Unattended**. Each mode has specific use cases depending on whether user interaction is needed or if the process can run autonomously.

1. Attended Flow

An **Attended flow** is designed for individual task automation where the user may need to interact at certain points, such as when a decision needs to be made.

- **Initiation:** Attended flows are triggered **on demand**, meaning the user manually starts them from their **local computer**.
- **User Interaction:** During the flow's execution, the user may need to provide input or intervene if required.
- **Sign-In Requirement:** The user must be signed in to their computer to run an attended desktop flow.

2. Unattended Flow

Unattended flows, on the other hand, are used for **high-volume automation** where no user interaction is needed. These flows are typically used for repetitive, rule-based tasks.

- **Initiation:** Unattended desktop flows are triggered by **cloud flows** in Power Automate. The cloud flow sets the necessary input variables and receives the output after the desktop flow completes.

- **No User Interaction:** These flows run fully autonomously without requiring any input or intervention from the user.

Important If a user is signed in, **unattended flows cannot run**. This is because the flow requires the user to be signed out, allowing the system to run the flow without any disruption.

Virtual Machines for Unattended Flows

For **unattended flows**, you have the option to use either the **user's computers** or **virtual machines** to execute the flows.

- **User's Computers:** One way to run unattended flows is to leverage the **user's computer** during off-hours (like overnight or weekends). However, this requires the user to sign out, and the software must be consistently configured across all machines.

- **Virtual Machines (VMs):** A more robust solution involves using **Azure virtual machines**. This method offers several benefits:

  - **Consistency:** The software configuration remains consistent across all virtual machines.

  - **Scalability:** You can easily scale the number of virtual machines to meet demand.

  - **Availability:** The flows can run during **working hours**, making them available for high-volume automation at any time.

If using **virtual machines**, as a **solution architect**, you'll need to

- Define the **specifications** for the virtual machines

- Determine the **costs** of running the virtual machines

- Set up **autoscaling rules** to optimize costs, reducing virtual machine usage when not needed and maximizing hardware productivity during peak usage

By choosing the right mode for your desktop flows, you can automate both simple tasks and large-scale processes efficiently while ensuring smooth operation with or without user involvement.

Process Mining in Power Automate

Process mining in Power Automate is a powerful tool that helps you better understand how your business processes are functioning. It provides data-driven insights into your operations, allowing you to identify inefficiencies and uncover areas where improvements can be made.

What Can Process Mining Do for You?

1. **Improve Operational Efficiency:** Process mining helps you spot **bottlenecks** in your processes, which can be addressed to **streamline operations** and increase productivity.

2. **Optimize Resources:** It identifies areas where **manual tasks** can be automated, enabling you to reallocate resources more effectively and reduce the need for human intervention in repetitive tasks.

3. **Enhance Customer Experience:** By eliminating process **pain points**, you can improve the overall **customer satisfaction** and create a smoother experience for your clients.

4. **Ensure Compliance:** Process mining helps detect **noncompliant processes**, so you can take **corrective actions** and minimize risks related to compliance issues.

As a **solution architect**, you should consider using process mining both during the **gathering requirements** phase and when **mapping business processes**. By connecting to your existing data sources, process mining gives you a visual map of how processes are currently running in your organization.

How It Works

- **Process mining** connects to data from various sources and generates a **visual process map** that helps you understand how business processes unfold across your organization. It provides a detailed view of the process flow and shows which activities take the longest, what variations exist, and where delays or bottlenecks are occurring.

- **Task mining** (a related feature) captures detailed steps of tasks performed on users' desktops. It records the actions involved in processes and provides visual maps for deeper analysis. Task mining also offers **guided recommendations** for potential automations based on what it observes.

Visualizing Your Processes

The **process map** is where you'll get the most value. It visually represents which activities are taking the most time and which variations of those activities are the most time-consuming. By spotting these **pain points** early, you can optimize the flow of work and ensure smoother operations across the board.

To unlock the full potential of these insights, it's helpful to integrate **Power BI**, which provides additional **visualizations** and **analytics**. This way, you can get a more comprehensive understanding of your processes and determine how best to improve them.

By leveraging **process mining** in Power Automate, you'll be able to make informed decisions that drive better performance, save time, and reduce costs while boosting the overall efficiency of your organization.

Introduction to Microsoft Copilot Studio and Agents

In today's world, communication happens across multiple channels like email, web chat, social media, and messaging platforms such as Slack, Microsoft Teams, and Facebook. For businesses, being accessible across these channels while maintaining a consistent response is crucial. Customers expect timely, personalized, and intelligent responses, and organizations need to deliver just that—no matter which channel the customer uses.

With the increasing demand for quick, tailored answers, organizations turn to **Conversational AI**—also known as agents. These agents can respond to customer or employee inquiries intelligently and handle common tasks across various platforms. The goal is to enable conversations, whether it's for resolving an issue, answering a question, or assisting in a transaction.

The Challenges of Building Agents

Creating an agent isn't without its challenges. Here are some statistics that highlight the issues organizations face:

- **66%** of customers prefer to use **self-service** options rather than contacting support due to the long wait times and time-consuming nature of speaking to support representatives.

- **90%** of customers expect consistent experiences across all channels. Whether interacting through phone, website, or a retail store, they want the same treatment everywhere.

- **59%** of communication channels operate in **silos**—call centers, websites, and retail stores each manage their systems separately, leading to disjointed customer experiences.

Building and maintaining agents traditionally involves a variety of skills: development for coding, subject matter experts (SMEs) to define conversational flows, AI specialists for language processing, and system integrations to connect the agent to relevant data. This process is often time-consuming and expensive.

Microsoft Copilot Studio

Enter **Microsoft Copilot Studio**. This platform allows anyone—whether they're business users, SMEs, or developers—to create powerful conversational agents. With **no-code** graphical interfaces, users can define the flow of conversations without needing to write a single line of code. Developers and admins can assist by integrating the agents into business applications using **Power Automate** flows.

The beauty of Microsoft Copilot Studio is that it combines language processing with a **low-cost, low-time solution** for creating and deploying conversational agents. Now, you don't need specialized technical skills to design an agent, which significantly reduces both time and cost.

Use Cases for Agents

Agents powered by Copilot Studio can be used in various ways to improve customer and employee experiences. Some of the **external use cases** for agents include

- Answering customer questions and inquiries
- Handling returns, exchanges, and complaints
- Assisting with purchases, checking inventory, making recommendations, or tracking shipments
- Providing help desk support and product introductions
- Making reservations or purchasing tickets

- Managing email preferences or processing claims
- Offering triage for healthcare and crisis communication
- Collecting customer feedback via surveys, quizzes, and contests

But agents aren't just for customer support. Internally, agents can streamline operations and improve productivity. Here are some **internal use cases**:

- HR support and employee onboarding
- Managing employee ideas and feedback
- IT support and sales support
- Case management and issue tracking
- Managing inspections and internal process information

Why Build Internal Agents?

Internal agents offer several key benefits:

- **Consistency in Communication:** Internal agents ensure that all employees get the same information, reducing confusion and improving alignment across teams.

- **Convenience and Speed:** Agents are available 24/7, meaning employees can access information or complete tasks at any time without waiting for human intervention.

- **Routine Task Automation:** Agents can handle repetitive tasks, freeing up employees to focus on more complex or higher-value activities.

- **Replacing Internal Systems:** An agent can replace the need for an intranet or internal email system, offering a faster and more efficient way to access frequently used information.

Solution Architect's Role in Deploying Agents

As a solution architect, you'll need to decide when and where agents should be implemented. For example, you might use agents to replace

- **Web forms** for lead generation or customer inquiries
- Navigating users to the right person or resource, instead of relying on a search feature
- Redirecting customer inquiries to the correct department, such as customer service or professional services

Agents aren't limited to just websites. With Microsoft Copilot Studio, you can deploy agents across various platforms like

- Facebook
- Slack
- Twilio
- Email
- Mobile apps
- MS Team Platform

Microsoft Copilot Licensing: It costs around 30$ per user per month if you pay yearly or 31$ per user per month if you pay monthly as of March 2025. It may be subject to change.

CHAPTER 4 LEVERAGING MICROSOFT COPILOT AND RPA AND SECURING DATA MODELS IN POWER PLATFORM SOLUTIONS

Microsoft Copilot enhances productivity across Microsoft 365 and the Power Platform by integrating AI-driven automation into applications like Word, Excel, PowerPoint, Outlook, Teams, and Power BI. It assists in drafting content, analyzing data, summarizing emails, automating workflows, and generating reports through natural language prompts. To use Copilot, organizations require a **Microsoft 365 Copilot license** and a compatible plan. Users can integrate Copilot with **Power Automate** for advanced workflows and **AI Builder** for custom AI solutions. Ensuring **data security and compliance** with **DLP policies** and **Microsoft Purview** is essential for governance. Copilot transforms business processes by streamlining tasks, improving decision-making, and driving efficiency.

Responsible AI Principles

As agents are AI-powered, it's crucial to follow **responsible AI principles** to ensure ethical and transparent usage. One key principle is **transparency**—making sure that users understand they are interacting with an agent. When a conversation begins, the agent should clearly state that it is an AI-driven entity, outline its capabilities, and mention any limitations. Additionally, agents should offer users an easy way to escalate or transfer the conversation to a human if needed.

It's also essential that agents are **purpose-driven**. They should be designed to address specific tasks or scenarios rather than trying to handle a broad range of topics. This focused approach helps ensure the conversation remains efficient and effective.

Agent Building Options: Choosing the Right Approach

Microsoft offers several powerful tools to help build conversational agents, each catering to different needs and levels of expertise. Whether you're a developer or a business user, there's an option for creating agents that can meet your organization's requirements.

1. Azure Bot Framework

The **Azure Bot Framework** is a robust set of SDKs and tools for developers to create custom agents and virtual assistants using code. It's part of the **Azure Bot Service**, which is a managed service for building and deploying bots.

- **How It Works:** Agents built using the Azure Bot Framework handle messages in a conversational "turn" system, similar to how humans take turns speaking in a conversation. An agent receives a message, processes it, and sends a response. This could involve accessing databases, calling APIs, reading files, or performing other operations.

- **Language Understanding:** With **Language Understanding (LUIS)**, agents can process and understand user language, making conversations feel more natural. You can also use **QnA Maker** to integrate a knowledge base into the agent for quicker responses.

- **Deployment and Channels:** Once an agent is built, it can be deployed across various communication channels, like **Facebook**, **Slack**, or **Teams**, without needing to modify the underlying code. The Azure Bot Service ensures that your agent adapts its responses to suit each channel's format.

- **Integration:** The Azure Bot Framework can also integrate with Microsoft Copilot Studio, allowing you to extend your agent's capabilities.

2. Bot Framework Composer

Bot Framework Composer is a tool that allows you to build agents using a **visual interface**. This tool simplifies the process by allowing you to design conversational flows without needing to write code.

- **Features**
    - A visual **editing canvas** to design conversation flows
    - Support for **LUIS** and **QnA Maker** to manage language understanding and knowledge bases
    - A **language generation system** and templates to make conversations feel more dynamic
    - A **runtime executable program** for testing your agent
- **How It Compares to Copilot Studio:** Like **Microsoft Copilot Studio**, Bot Framework Composer provides a no-code experience for users to build agents. However, it offers more flexibility and customization for developers, allowing for deeper control over the agent's functionality. It's an open source, cross-platform tool that works on **Windows**, **Linux**, and **macOS**.
- **Customization:** You can also create custom content in **Bot Framework Composer** and import it into **Microsoft Copilot Studio** for further development.

3. Microsoft Copilot Studio

Microsoft Copilot Studio is designed for business users, subject matter experts (SMEs), and anyone looking to build agents without coding experience. This tool uses a **no-code** graphical interface, making it easy to create and deploy agents quickly.

- **Key Features**
    - **No-Code Creation:** Build agents directly in your web browser without any programming knowledge.
    - **AI-Powered Interactions:** Copilot Studio agents use AI to handle repetitive, simple tasks, freeing up time for more complex work.
    - **Multichannel Deployment:** You can deploy these agents on various platforms such as **your website**, **Facebook**, or **Microsoft Teams**.
    - **Built for SMEs:** It's specifically designed to allow SMEs to create agents without needing data scientists or developers.
- **Technology Stack:** Copilot Studio is built on top of the Azure Bot Framework, leveraging its capabilities in a no-code environment. It's designed for users who need to address straightforward requirements for internal or external agents.
- **Licensing:** To build agents with Microsoft Copilot Studio, you'll need both a **tenant license** and a **user license**.

Choosing the Right Tool for Your Needs

When deciding which agent technology to use, solution architects must consider several factors:

- **Skill Set:** Do you have a team of developers, or are you working with business users who need a no-code solution?

- **Existing Solutions:** Are there already agents in place that you need to extend or integrate with new solutions?

- **Complexity:** How complex are the agents you need? If you need highly customized and sophisticated agents, tools like the **Azure Bot Framework** or **Bot Framework Composer** might be the best fit. If your needs are simpler, **Microsoft Copilot Studio** could be more than sufficient.

Each tool has its own strengths and is suited to different types of users and requirements. Whether you're building a simple FAQ bot for your website or a complex virtual assistant integrated with backend systems, Microsoft offers a range of solutions that can help you achieve your goals efficiently and effectively.

Key Concepts for Building Agents

Before diving into building your agent, there are some important concepts to understand that will guide you through the process of creating effective, natural, and functional conversational agents.

1. Language Understanding

For an agent to communicate effectively with humans, it needs to understand the language in a natural way. When users interact with an application, they don't speak the application's internal code; they use everyday language. That's where **Natural Language Processing (NLP)** comes in.

NLP enables the agent to understand human language and respond accordingly. **Microsoft Copilot Studio** leverages NLP through the **Language Understanding (LUIS)** service, a part of **Azure Cognitive Services**. This allows your agents to understand text or speech and react to user input in a way that feels natural.

- **How It Works:** Microsoft Copilot Studio uses an advanced NLP model that is **transformer based**, making it easy to create agents without needing AI experts. This model learns from large amounts of data, making it capable of handling new tasks with just a few examples and minimal training.

- **Benefits:** With the language understanding model, agent builders can focus on creating conversational flows without delving deeply into AI concepts, making it more accessible for nontechnical users.

2. Topics

In Microsoft Copilot Studio, the **topics** define the main subjects or areas of conversation that your agent can handle. Think of topics as the building blocks of your agent's conversational flow.

- **How It Works:** When a user interacts with the agent, the agent needs to identify what the user is asking about—this is where topics come in. Each topic has a set of **trigger phrases** (user input that signals the agent to respond in a specific way) and **conversation nodes** (which define how the agent responds to the user).

- **Example:** If your agent is designed to answer questions about your product, one topic might be "Product Information" with trigger phrases like "Tell me about the product" or "What is the product made of?" The conversation node will dictate how the agent should respond, such as pulling up product details.

- **How to Create Topics:** You only need a few examples (usually five to ten) for trigger phrases, and shorter phrases are better for training. The NLP model is capable of understanding variations in the phrasing, so you don't have to worry about minor changes like adding articles or changing plural forms.

- **Generate Topics:** If you have existing documents, product info, FAQs, or procedures, Copilot Studio can extract relevant topics automatically by using its **Suggest Topics** feature. It can even pull topics from **Microsoft Dynamics 365 Customer Service Insights**.

3. Entities

An **entity** refers to specific pieces of information that can be extracted from user input, such as names, dates, or quantities. This allows your agent to tailor its responses based on what the user provides.

- **How It Works:** When a user types something like "Schedule a meeting for tomorrow at 3 PM," the agent can extract the date ("tomorrow") and time ("3 PM") as entities to help decide the next step in the conversation.

- **Prebuilt and Custom Entities:** Copilot Studio comes with a set of **prebuilt entities** for common items like dates, numbers, and locations. However, you can also create **custom entities** that are specific to your business domain, such as product names, project codes, or customer IDs.

4. Channels

Once you've built your agent, you need to think about how users will interact with it. **Channels** are the platforms or services through which users can communicate with your agent.

- **Azure Bot Framework** allows you to develop an agent once and then deploy it across multiple channels without changing the underlying code. This makes it easy to expand your agent's reach.

- **Available Channels:** You can connect your agent to various platforms, such as
  - Microsoft Teams
  - Facebook
  - Slack
  - Skype
  - Twilio (SMS)
  - Web Chat
  - Alexa
  - Email and more

CHAPTER 4　LEVERAGING MICROSOFT COPILOT AND RPA AND SECURING DATA MODELS IN POWER PLATFORM SOLUTIONS

- **Deploying Copilot Studio:** Just like with Azure Bot Framework, **Microsoft Copilot Studio** can be deployed across these channels, ensuring your agent is available where your users are.

By understanding these key concepts—**Language Understanding**, **Topics**, **Entities**, and **Channels**—you can effectively design agents that offer natural, meaningful conversations and are adaptable to a variety of use cases and platforms. Whether you are building a basic FAQ bot or a more complex conversational assistant, these foundational elements will ensure that your agent is intuitive, flexible, and capable of handling a wide range of user interactions.

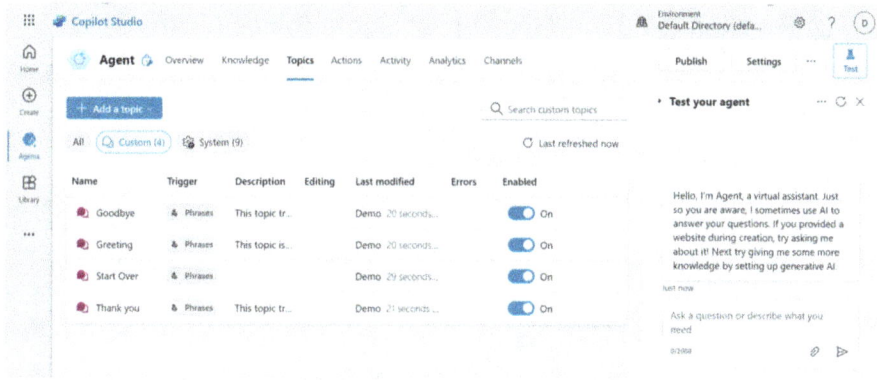

Figure 4-1. *Copilot Topics*

CHAPTER 4 LEVERAGING MICROSOFT COPILOT AND RPA AND SECURING DATA MODELS IN POWER PLATFORM SOLUTIONS

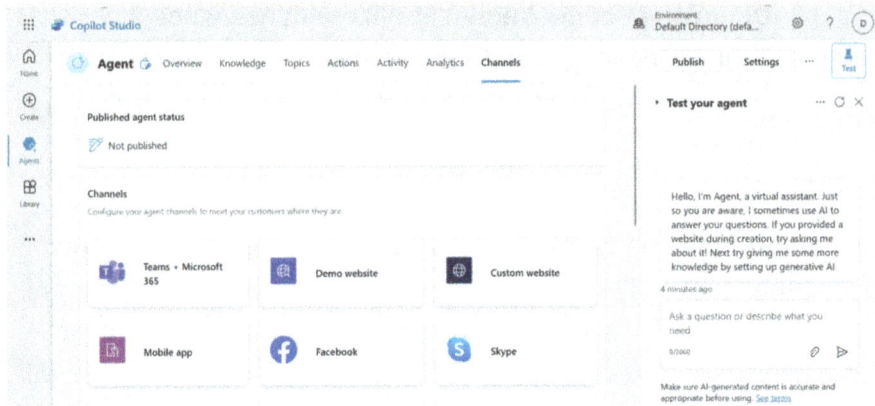

***Figure 4-2.** Copilot Channels*

Figures 4-1 and 4-2 show the Copilot Studio Topics and Channels; explore more Copilot and other features with free trial using your company or school account and explore Microsoft Learn modules to learn more about these features and functionality.

Data Modeling and Security for Power Platform Solutions

Introduction

Let's face it—security often gets overlooked until it's too late. You've probably seen it happen: a solution is nearly complete, and someone suddenly realizes, "Wait, what about security?" The scramble begins, and before you know it, the project faces delays, unexpected costs, or worse—a poorly implemented security model.

Here's the thing: **security isn't just a box to check; it's a critical part of your Power Platform solution's design.** As a solution architect, your role is to think ahead and bake security into your solution right from the start. Why? Because getting it right early on saves you from significant headaches later.

CHAPTER 4 LEVERAGING MICROSOFT COPILOT AND RPA AND SECURING DATA MODELS IN POWER PLATFORM SOLUTIONS

In this chapter, we'll dive deep into **data modeling and security**, helping you master the art of balancing two vital aspects of every solution:

1. **User Access:** Ensuring people can get the information and tools they need to do their jobs

2. **System Security:** Keeping data safe, compliant, and out of the wrong hands

A great security strategy is all about finding that balance. Too lax, and your data is at risk—potentially unreliable, or worse, exposed. Too strict, and you might stifle productivity as users look for workarounds to get their jobs done. Either extreme can lead to low adoption, and we all know that if users don't embrace the solution, it doesn't matter how well it's built.

Why Security Matters More Than Ever

Let's put it into perspective:

- **Data drives businesses.** It's a critical asset, and losing control of it—whether to a competitor or due to noncompliance—can be disastrous.

- **Regulations are everywhere.** From GDPR to HIPAA, organizations must stay compliant, or they'll face hefty fines and reputational damage.

- **Trust is key.** If users don't feel confident in the system's data or access controls, adoption rates plummet.

As a solution architect, you need to go beyond knowing that security is important. You have to lead the charge in designing a security model that works for everyone—balancing usability, compliance, and protection.

Security Architecture: A Step-by-Step Approach

We'll explore how to

- Discover your client's unique security requirements, including **authentication** (like SSO and multifactor authentication), **network security**, and **data retention policies**.

- Map security needs to Power Platform features, creating blueprints for **authorization, app-level entitlements**, and **data access policies**.

- Advocate for **simplicity and scalability** when designing security layers for apps, data, and processes.

The Power Platform gives you plenty of tools to get the job done, but it's up to you to use them wisely. Whether you're designing security for apps, columns, or entire business processes, this chapter will show you how to keep your solution secure, user-friendly, and compliant—without overcomplicating things.

Ready to learn how to make security a strong foundation of your Power Platform solutions? Let's get started!

Common Data Model – A Solution Architect's Essential Tool for Data Interoperability

As a solution architect, understanding the Common Data Model (CDM) is crucial for ensuring seamless data interoperability across various business applications. In this chapter, we will explore the foundational aspects of CDM, its features, and how it fits into Microsoft's broader ecosystem to facilitate effective and scalable business solutions.

What Is the Common Data Model?

The Common Data Model defines a universal language for business entities that span the core areas of sales, services, marketing, operations, finance, talent, and commerce. It provides a common framework for the customer, people, and product entities that drive business processes across organizations. The goal of CDM is to enable data and application interoperability that transcends multiple systems, service implementations, and vendors.

CDM ensures that data is self-describing, meaning that applications can read, interpret, and understand the data without complex configurations. This is accomplished by using well-defined schemas (or structures) that describe the relationships, attributes, and entities that make up business data.

Key Features of the Common Data Model

The Common Data Model is not just a single schema but a standardized and extensible collection of schemas. Let's look at some of the core features:

- **Unified Data Definition:** CDM allows various applications and data integrators to work together by providing a unified definition of data, making integration across platforms smoother and more efficient.

- **Rich Metadata System:** The model includes a comprehensive set of entities, relationships, hierarchies, and traits, offering a flexible foundation for different business processes.

- **Open Source and Extensible:** Originally developed from Microsoft Dynamics 365/CRM apps, CDM is now open source and available on GitHub. With over 260 standard entities, it offers broad applicability for businesses of all types.

- **Wide Adoption:** Various systems and platforms, such as Dataverse, Microsoft Power BI dataflows, Microsoft Azure data services, and Informatica, all implement the Common Data Model. This wide implementation ensures that CDM is foundational in enabling data interoperability across systems.

How Is the Common Data Model Used?

CDM is integral to several Microsoft platforms and tools, particularly when provisioning a Dataverse environment. Here's a deeper look at where CDM is used:

- **Dataverse Environment:** When you provision a Dataverse environment, the core schema from CDM automatically creates the tables, columns, and relationships within the Dataverse database. Common core tables include *Account, Contact, Lead,* and *Task.* These foundational tables are used to represent key business concepts that span multiple business processes.

- **Dynamics 365 Apps:** When deploying applications such as Dynamics 365 Sales, tables are created from the core schema, CRM base schema, and industry-specific schema (Sales schema). This ensures that data across multiple apps is consistently structured, helping businesses achieve better data integration and reporting.

- **Integration with Other Tools:** The storage format defined by CDM is used in tools like Microsoft Power BI, Azure Data Factory, and Power Automate. This ensures that various platforms can share and process data in a standardized way, enabling interoperability and simplifying the creation of enterprise solutions.

Industry Accelerators in Microsoft's Ecosystem

For organizations in industry-specific verticals, the Common Data Model is extended with predefined schemas through Microsoft Industry Accelerators. These accelerators help businesses rapidly build solutions by adding new entities specific to their industry's needs. These accelerators enhance CDM by incorporating specialized data models and relationships.

Microsoft's Industry Accelerators support a variety of industries:

- **Automotive:** For manufacturers, dealers, and service providers in the automotive industry, the accelerator includes entities and data structures specific to vehicle sales, service, and maintenance.

- **Financial Services:** Includes data models for banking, insurance, and investment services, enabling organizations in this industry to build solutions faster and with more accuracy.

- **Education:** CDM accelerators for education support both K–12 schools and higher education institutions by structuring data on students, faculty, courses, and learning management systems.

- **Nonprofit:** This accelerator supports nonprofit organizations by creating models that facilitate donor management, fundraising campaigns, volunteer tracking, and other core activities of nonprofits.

- **Manufacturing:** With manufacturing-specific data models, CDM helps in managing production processes, inventory tracking, supply chain management, and other critical manufacturing operations.

- **Media and Entertainment:** The accelerator supports entities and relationships tailored to the media and entertainment sector, such as content creation, distribution, and audience engagement.

By using industry accelerators, solution architects can leverage prebuilt entities and relationships, reducing the time and effort required to design solutions for specific industries.

Benefits of Common Data Model

The benefits of adopting CDM are numerous and impactful, especially when it comes to ensuring data consistency, improving interoperability, and reducing integration challenges. Some of the key advantages include

- **Improved Data Integration:** By providing a standardized schema, CDM allows businesses to integrate data across various systems seamlessly. This is essential in today's environment, where businesses rely on multiple systems to manage different functions.

- **Reduced Complexity:** CDM's predefined entities and relationships minimize the need for custom data models, reducing complexity and speeding up the development process.

- **Faster Solution Deployment:** By using the industry accelerators and standard schemas in CDM, solution architects can deploy solutions more quickly without reinventing the wheel.

- **Scalability:** CDM's extensibility allows organizations to scale their data models as their business grows, ensuring that the solution remains relevant as business processes evolve.

CHAPTER 4 LEVERAGING MICROSOFT COPILOT AND RPA AND SECURING DATA MODELS IN POWER PLATFORM SOLUTIONS

Data Modeling in Microsoft Power Platform: Designing Effective Data Architectures

As a solution architect, one of your critical roles is designing data models that ensure the seamless flow, storage, and management of information across various systems. In the context of Microsoft Power Platform, data modeling is a pivotal part of the solution design, ensuring that data is organized and structured in ways that maximize efficiency, usability, and scalability.

What Is Data Modeling?

Data modeling is the process of designing and structuring data to ensure that it aligns with business processes and technical requirements. On Microsoft Power Platform, this involves defining data structures in tools like **Dataverse** and **Azure Data Lake** and integrating data from external sources through **connectors**.

While different standards for data modeling exist (e.g., Unified Modeling Language [UML], IDEF1X), we'll focus on data modeling within Dataverse and how it connects various data stores.

Types of Data Models

In the context of Dataverse, data models generally fall into two primary categories:

- Logical Data Models
- Physical Data Models

Additionally, **Entity Relationship Diagrams (ERDs)** and **Object Diagrams** are also key components of data modeling.

Logical Data Models

A logical data model provides a high-level view of how data flows through the system. These models are often created early in the project, typically during the discovery phase, before the full schema (columns, entities) is finalized.

Key Characteristics of Logical Data Models

- **High-Level Abstraction:** Focuses on entities and their relationships, not on how data is physically stored.

- **Business Names:** Entities are often referred to by their business terms (e.g., *Customer*, *Order*), not by their technical schema names.

- **Data Flow Focus:** Shows the movement of data across systems, helping teams understand how data is transferred and processed without focusing on implementation details.

Example: A logical data model for managing customer relationships might show entities such as *Customer*, *Order*, and *Product*, along with their relationships, without specifying exact table structures or columns.

Physical Data Models

In contrast, physical data models are much more granular and detailed. They provide an in-depth representation of how data is actually implemented within the system.

Key Characteristics of Physical Data Models

- **Column-Level Details:** Specifies the exact columns for each table, including data types, constraints, and other properties

CHAPTER 4 LEVERAGING MICROSOFT COPILOT AND RPA AND SECURING DATA MODELS IN POWER PLATFORM SOLUTIONS

- **System Implementation:** Includes Dataverse, Azure Data Lake, or other data storage solutions, detailing how the data is physically stored and accessed

- **Design Relationships:** Focuses on how tables are linked and the specific details of those relationships, such as primary keys and foreign keys

Example: A physical data model for a sales order system might include tables for *Customer*, *Order*, and *Payment*, along with columns such as *OrderID*, *CustomerName*, and *PaymentMethod*, alongside their associated relationships.

Entity Relationship Diagrams (ERDs)

Entity Relationship Diagrams (ERDs) visually represent the relationships between entities in a database. They help teams understand how different pieces of data are interconnected and highlight important attributes.

Example: An ERD for a sales system might show a *Customer* entity connected to *Order* entities, with foreign keys representing the relationships.

Object Diagrams

Object diagrams provide a snapshot of what data needs to be visible and, equally important, what should remain hidden. They are typically created during modeling sessions with domain experts to help identify critical data elements and relationships.

Example: An object diagram might highlight specific details about a *Customer* object that need to be visible in the app, such as the *CustomerID* and *Email*, while hiding less critical data like internal *AccountBalance*.

Data Modeling Strategies

When building a data model for Dataverse and the broader Power Platform ecosystem, it's important to follow best practices to ensure both efficiency and clarity.

1. Start with Core Tables and Relationships

Don't get overwhelmed by the entire system at once. Focus on key entities and their relationships first, and gradually build out the rest of the data model. By solving small parts of the problem first, you'll be able to construct a more manageable and understandable model.

2. Avoid Over-normalization

It's tempting for teams with strong data architecture backgrounds to over-normalize the data model, treating Dataverse like a traditional SQL Server database. This can result in a poor user experience, extra processing requirements, and unnecessary complexity. Strive for a balance between normalization and usability.

3. Focus on Current Needs

While it's important to keep future requirements in mind, data modeling in Dataverse can be done incrementally. Take an agile approach and focus on the current needs, building a solid foundation that can be iterated upon in the future.

4. Leverage Proof of Concept

Dataverse allows you to create environments and test models quickly. If you're unsure about a particular approach, build a proof of concept, test it out, and refine it based on feedback. Challenge teams with the same problem to get diverse perspectives and solutions.

Factors Influencing Data Models

Several factors can influence how you structure your data model, from security requirements to user experience considerations.

1. Security Requirements

Security is a key consideration when designing data models. Solution architects should aim for simplification but must also be aware of security constraints that could impact the structure of the model. Some data may need to be encrypted, or access controls might need to be applied to certain entities.

2. User Experience

As you design the data model, keep in mind the impact on the user experience. Adding too many relationships or normalization layers can complicate how users navigate the system. Ensure that the data model is intuitive and aligns with the way users will interact with the application.

3. Data Location and Retention

Understand where data is stored and how long it needs to be retained. Certain data types may have regulatory requirements, such as personally identifiable information (PII), that dictate how and where they should be stored. Dataverse and Azure provide features to comply with these regulations.

4. Self-Service Reporting

Power BI and other tools depend on self-service reporting. If the data model is overly complex, users may struggle to build reports on their own. Aim to create a model that allows for easy navigation, especially for those who aren't database experts.

5. Integration with Existing Systems

Consider the systems you are integrating with. Are they legacy systems? Do they have APIs? How will you access or copy the data? The data model must accommodate these integration requirements.

6. Localization

If the solution needs to support multiple regions, languages, or currencies, the data model must be able to handle these requirements. Ensure that your model accounts for multilingual and multicurrency needs, including translations and region-specific data storage.

Choosing the Right Data Store for Your Microsoft Power Platform Apps

When designing solutions using Microsoft Power Platform, one of the critical decisions you'll need to make is where to store your data. The choice of data store depends on several factors, including whether you're working with new or existing data, how you intend to use the data, and the level of integration required with other systems. This chapter explores the various data storage options and provides guidelines for selecting the most appropriate data store for your app.

Data Stores in Microsoft Power Platform

Microsoft Power Platform offers various options for storing and managing data, each suited for different scenarios. These options include **Dataverse**, **Azure Data Lake**, **Connectors**, **Dataflows**, and **Virtual Tables**.

Dataverse

Dataverse is the core data storage option for Microsoft Power Platform and is ideal for apps that need to manage transactional data. It provides a unified, secure data store that abstracts the complexities of the underlying data storage technology, enabling apps to access and manipulate data efficiently.

- **Use Cases:** Dataverse is best suited for apps that require data to be created, read, updated, and deleted (CRUD operations). It is especially effective when your app needs to work with structured, relational data.

- **Storage:** Dataverse stores data in a combination of Microsoft Azure SQL Database, Azure Cosmos DB, and Azure Storage.

- **Integration:** Dataverse is integrated with Power Apps, Power Automate, Power Virtual Agents, and Power BI, enabling seamless access to data across the platform.

When to Use Dataverse

1. **New Data:** If your app is creating new data that doesn't already exist or was previously managed through manual processes (e.g., paper-based systems), Dataverse is an excellent choice for storing and managing that data.

2. **Transactional Data:** For managing transactional data that will be consumed and manipulated by your apps, such as customer information, orders, and invoices.

3. **High Availability:** When you need a scalable and reliable data store that supports high availability and disaster recovery.

Azure Data Lake

Azure Data Lake is a storage service that is designed for large-scale data storage, particularly for unstructured or semi-structured data.

- **Use Cases:** Azure Data Lake is ideal for storing large volumes of data that might be difficult to store in traditional relational databases. It's particularly suited for storing data from external systems, performing analytics, and working with large datasets that require complex processing.

- **Storage:** Azure Data Lake is optimized for storing structured, semi-structured, and unstructured data. It allows you to store data in its native format and supports high-throughput analytics.

When to Use Azure Data Lake

1. **External System Data:** If you need to store data from external sources (e.g., third-party services or legacy systems) and need to perform analytics or batch processing on it.

2. **Read-Focused Data:** For scenarios where data is read more frequently than it is written, such as large datasets used for reporting, analytics, and data science.

3. **Common Data Model Structure:** When you need to structure the data in a **Common Data Model** format, which is useful for standardizing data across different systems.

CHAPTER 4   LEVERAGING MICROSOFT COPILOT AND RPA AND SECURING DATA MODELS IN POWER PLATFORM SOLUTIONS

Connectors

Connectors allow you to connect your app to external data sources such as **SharePoint**, **SQL Server**, **Microsoft 365**, and other third-party systems.

- **Use Cases:** Connectors are ideal when you want to leave existing data where it resides and simply connect to those data sources from within Power Platform apps.

- **Integration:** Connectors make it easy to pull data from existing systems without the need to copy it into another data store.

When to Use Connectors

1. **Read/Write from Existing Systems:** If your app needs to access live data from an existing system (e.g., SQL Server or SharePoint) and perform CRUD operations, connectors are the right choice.

2. **Data That Should Remain in Place:** If you don't need to store or replicate the data elsewhere but just need access to it in real time.

Dataflows

Dataflows are used to extract, transform, and load (ETL) data from external systems into Dataverse or Azure Data Lake.

- **Use Cases:** Dataflows are particularly useful when you need to pull data from multiple sources, transform it (e.g., cleanse, format, or aggregate), and store it in a central location.

- **Data Processing:** Unlike connectors, which provide real-time access to data, dataflows are typically used for batch processing, where data is fetched on a scheduled basis.

When to Use Dataflows

1. **Data Transformation:** When you need to extract data from various sources, transform it (e.g., data cleansing, formatting), and load it into a central store like Dataverse.

2. **Scheduled Updates:** If your app doesn't need live data but requires periodic updates from external systems, dataflows are an ideal choice.

Virtual Tables

Virtual tables provide a way to integrate external data sources with Dataverse in a way that makes the data appear as if it is stored within Dataverse, while actually residing in an external database.

- **Use Cases:** Virtual tables are used when you want to expose external data (e.g., from an Azure SQL Database) in a way that users can interact with it just like regular Dataverse tables.

- **Integration:** Data is fetched from external databases on-demand via APIs but behaves as though it's part of Dataverse.

When to Use Virtual Tables

1. **External Data:** When you need to access and interact with data from an external source (e.g., an Azure SQL Database) without physically moving the data into Dataverse.

2. **Read/Write from External Systems:** Virtual tables allow read and write operations on external data, which makes them more flexible than connectors in some scenarios.

Choosing Where to Store Data

To determine the most appropriate data store for your solution, consider the following factors:

1. **New Data:** If your app is creating new data (e.g., a new process that replaces a paper-based workflow), store the data in **Dataverse** for transactional management.

2. **Existing Data:** If you need to access or manipulate data that already exists in another system, use **connectors** to pull or push data from external systems in real time.

3. **Copy of Existing Data:** If you need to work with data from an external system but ensure that the original data is not modified, use **Virtual Tables** or **Dataflows** to replicate and work with the data without changing the source system.

4. **Large Data:** If your app requires working with large volumes of data, such as logs or data for analytics, **Azure Data Lake** is the best option for storing and processing large, unstructured datasets.

By evaluating the nature of the data and how your app will interact with it, you can select the right data store to optimize your solution's performance and scalability.

CHAPTER 4   LEVERAGING MICROSOFT COPILOT AND RPA AND SECURING DATA MODELS IN POWER PLATFORM SOLUTIONS

Data Model: Environment Security

Environments in Microsoft Power Platform act as containers for managing apps, flows, connections, and other resources. These environments also allow administrators to control user access to these resources. It is important to note that access to apps in Power Apps or flows in Power Automate does not automatically grant users access to all data. Users can only access the data they are authorized to access.

Access to environments is multilayered, starting with the Microsoft Entra ID tenant. For users to access an environment, they must have a Microsoft Entra ID account and a Power Platform license. If a Dataverse database is available in the environment, users will need a Dataverse security role. If no Dataverse database is present, users will need a Microsoft 365 role to access the environment. Additionally, users must be granted permission on specific resources within the environment, such as apps, flows, and connectors.

Administrators also have the ability to control access to environments from other Microsoft Entra ID tenants in business-to-business (B2B) scenarios.

Microsoft Entra ID Authentication

Power Platform uses Microsoft Entra ID for user authentication. Microsoft Entra ID provides various features that help manage and secure access:

- **Identity and Access Management:** Manages access to Power Apps
- **Authentication:** Verifies user credentials for apps with multiple users in a flow
- **Single Sign-On (SSO):** Allows users to access apps without needing to sign in multiple times

- **Multifactor Authentication (MFA):** Adds an additional layer of verification when signing in

- **Business-to-Business (B2B):** Allows guest and external partner access while maintaining control over organizational data

- **Conditional Access:** Controls app access based on factors like user, device, and location

- **Device Management:** Manages device access to corporate data

- **Enterprise Users:** Handles license assignments

- **Hybrid Identity:** Supports unified authentication across cloud and on-premises services

- **Identity Governance:** Manages access controls for employees, business partners, and apps

- **Identity Protection:** Detects vulnerabilities in user identities

- **Reports and Monitoring:** Provides insights into security and usage patterns

Unsupported Features

Certain Microsoft Entra ID features are currently not supported by Power Platform:

- **Business-to-Consumer (B2C):** Power Platform does not support customer sign-ins via social or enterprise accounts.

- **Managed Identities:** Power Platform does not support managed identities; service principals are required instead.

- **Privileged Identity Management (PIM):** Just-in-time administrator access is not supported in Power Platform.

Conditional Access

With Microsoft Entra ID Premium, organizations can create **Conditional Access** policies. These policies control access based on user, device, and location. This ensures that only authorized users can access Power Platform apps and data.

B2B Collaboration

For B2B scenarios, Microsoft Entra ID allows organizations to invite guest users to collaborate on apps created in Power Platform. Guest users can access these apps but cannot create or edit Power Apps. To enable guest access, licenses must be assigned to them for app usage.

Cross-Tenant Isolation

Cross-tenant isolation enhances security by restricting the sharing of apps and data between tenants. By default, each tenant can access resources from another tenant, but cross-tenant isolation can restrict access.

- **Outbound Restrictions:** Blocks users in your tenant from connecting to external resources
- **Inbound Restrictions:** Blocks users from external tenants from accessing your tenant's resources

Security Groups and Environment Access

To control access to environments, administrators can associate **Microsoft Entra ID security groups** with the environments. When a security group is associated, only users in that group will have access to the environment.

- Users outside the security group will be disabled in Dataverse if the group is linked to an environment.

- If no security group is linked, all users with a Power Apps license will be enabled in the environment.

- Note that distribution groups and Office 365 groups cannot be linked to environments.

Roles and Administration

There are several administrative roles for managing environments and performing administrative tasks:

- **Microsoft Power Platform Admin:** Can create and manage environments, manage Power Apps, Power Automate, and Data Loss Prevention policies

- **Delegated Admin:** Used by CSP partners to manage services for their customers

- **Environment Admin:** Manages environments without Dataverse and can assign users the Environment Maker role

When a Dataverse database is present, the **Environment Admin** role is combined with the **System Administrator** security role in Dataverse, and the **Environment Maker** role gets the **Basic User** security role.

Data Loss Prevention (DLP)

Data Loss Prevention (DLP) policies in Microsoft Power Platform play a crucial role in securing organizational data. These policies act as guardrails to help prevent unintentional exposure of sensitive information and protect the overall information security within the tenant. DLP policies enforce rules that define which connectors are enabled for each environment and determine which connectors can be used together.

As a solution architect, understanding DLP policies is essential because

- DLPs ensure proper data flow within an organization, adhering to the organization's policies.

- If DLPs are not considered during solution development, they can prevent a solution from functioning properly.

- DLP policies can also disrupt a deployed solution if they are added after the deployment.

Key Facts about DLP Policies

1. **Enforcing Rules on Connectors:** DLP policies enforce rules that determine which connectors can be used together in apps and flows.

2. **Connector Classification:** Connectors are classified into groups:

    - **Business Data Only:** Can only be used with other connectors in the same group.

    - **No Business Data Allowed:** Cannot be used in flows or apps that involve business data.

- **Blocked:** These connectors cannot be used.

3. **Policy Application:** Tenant administrators can define DLP policies that apply to all environments. By default, no DLP policies are enforced in the tenant.

4. **Dataverse Connectors:** Dataverse connectors cannot be blocked by DLP policies.

DLP Policies and Environments

DLP policies can be applied at both the **tenant level** and the **environment level**:

- **Tenant-Level DLP Policies:** Apply to all environments within the tenant

- **Environment-Level DLP Policies:** Specific to individual environments, ensuring that each environment's data security requirements are met

You can apply multiple DLP policies to a single environment. At both design and runtime, all applicable policies for the environment are evaluated together. The most restrictive policy among the multiple policies will apply to the combination of connectors in the app or flow.

Important Notes

- Environment DLP policies cannot override tenant-wide DLP policies.

- It is recommended to minimize the number of policies and avoid applying multiple policies to the same environment.

Recommended Approach for Defining DLP Policies

1. **Default Policy:** Create a policy that applies to all environments, blocking unsupported non-Microsoft connectors and classifying all Microsoft connectors as business data.

2. **Training Environments:** For default and other training environments, create a more restrictive policy that further defines which Microsoft connectors can be classified as business data.

3. **Special Use Cases:** For specific environments, allow exceptions where certain connectors can be used as required.

Deploying DLP Policies

When deploying DLP policies, solution architects should consider the following:

- **Early Policy Establishment:** It's best to establish a default policy early and then grant exceptions as needed.

- **Impact of Restrictions:** New or updated restrictions can disable existing apps and flows.

- **Policy Propagation Delay:** Changes may take a few minutes to take effect.

- **Policy Application at Environment Level:** Policies can only be applied at the tenant or environment level, not at the user level.

- **Managing Policies:** DLP policies can be managed using Microsoft PowerShell or admin connectors.

- **User Visibility:** Users of resources in environments can view the policies that apply to them.

Collaboration with IT Groups

When deploying DLP policies to an existing tenant, solution architects should coordinate with other IT groups to

- Confirm that DLP policies support the planned deliverables

- Understand the lead time for approval and implementation of changes

- Clarify what actions the solution architect can take and what actions require collaboration with other IT teams

By using Microsoft Entra ID security groups, administrators can further control access to environments and resources, ensuring that only authorized users and applications can interact with sensitive data.

Access to Dataverse

In any system, data is a fundamental asset, and securing it properly is of utmost importance. For Dynamics 365 and Power Platform solutions, **Dataverse** is the underlying data platform, storing and managing data. However, just securing the access to Dataverse isn't enough. The real challenge lies in controlling who can access what data and how we manage those permissions. Let's delve deeper into Dataverse's security architecture.

CHAPTER 4   LEVERAGING MICROSOFT COPILOT AND RPA AND SECURING DATA MODELS
             IN POWER PLATFORM SOLUTIONS

Security Design Overview

Security is not merely about locking down systems. It's about creating a model that ensures data is used properly while protecting it from unauthorized access. The default security model for Dataverse controls access at multiple layers, both at the environment level and within the database. A solution architect needs to design the security model that can appropriately handle the data access requirements, ensuring performance, manageability, usability, and visibility.

Key Design Considerations

When designing security, a solution architect must understand that different business requirements dictate how security should be applied. Common patterns observed in security design across business applications include

- **Active Involvement:** Individuals who directly engage with customers/data

- **Secondary Involvement:** Support roles who monitor or advise but do not engage directly

- **Transactional Interaction:** Access to data for single or temporary tasks, such as in call centers

- **Management Oversight:** Supervisory roles with broad access to direct and indirect data

- **Reporting:** Data access for generating business reports without directly accessing sensitive information

- **Compliance:** Read-only access for audit purposes

By understanding the roles and workflows of users within the business, the architect can craft a security design that aligns with these requirements.

Design Principles

When establishing the security model, the solution architect must adhere to some critical principles:

1. **Assigned Responsibility Doesn't Always Need Restricted Access:** Just because a user is responsible for a task doesn't mean they need total access to the associated data.

2. **Treat Exceptions As Exceptions:** Most access patterns are common, and exceptions should be handled thoughtfully without complicating the design.

3. **You Can't Revoke Access to a Single Record:** If a user has access to a broad dataset, you can't selectively revoke access to just one record.

4. **Leverage Business Units:** For better manageability and security containment, business units are invaluable.

5. **Simplify Designs for Performance and Maintenance:** The simplest model that fulfills the requirements will generally offer the best performance.

Security Features in Dataverse

Dataverse offers a variety of security features that work together to ensure a robust access control system:

- **Table Ownership:** Determines the ownership of rows and grants access accordingly
- **Teams:** Groups of users that share access rights, simplifying permission management
- **Security Roles:** Define what actions a user or team can perform on data
- **Business Units:** Define boundaries for data access and allow granular control over data visibility
- **Sharing:** A mechanism for giving specific users or teams access to rows they wouldn't otherwise be able to access
- **Microsoft Entra ID Security Groups:** Allows integration with Azure AD security groups to manage access
- **Column-Level Security:** Protects sensitive data at the column level
- **Hierarchical Security:** Provides oversight at different management levels, useful for organizations with varying reporting structures

Table Ownership

Tables in Dataverse can either be **User/Team owned** or **Organization owned**. A **User/Team owned** table allows granular control of access at the row level. On the other hand, **Organization owned** tables allow access to all rows (or none), offering no granularity.

When creating tables, always consider **User/Team ownership**, as it allows greater flexibility.

Teams and Security Roles

Teams play a vital role in managing security. By grouping users, you can assign permissions to entire teams rather than individual users. This helps simplify management, particularly when scaling the solution.

There are three types of teams:

- **Owner Teams:** Teams that own rows of data.

- **Access Teams:** Teams that allow users to share specific rows of data.

- **Microsoft Entra ID Group Teams:** Membership is dynamically assigned from Azure AD groups.

Security Roles

Security roles are central to controlling access in Dataverse. Instead of assigning individual privileges, a security role groups multiple privileges together, which are then assigned to users or teams.

Business Units

Business units in Dataverse allow for the horizontal partitioning of data. You can think of them as security containers that group users and data. Each environment has a single root business unit, and additional child business units can be created to represent different departments, regions, or business divisions. This ensures data access is restricted based on the role and business unit hierarchy.

Important Notes on Business Units

- Business units provide efficient access management.
- Don't design business units solely based on the organization's chart. Instead, focus on security requirements.
- Users belong to one business unit at a time, but they can be members of multiple teams in different units.

Column-Level Security

While **row-level security** is critical, sometimes you need more granular control. Dataverse supports **column-level security**, allowing administrators to restrict access to specific columns in a table. For example, if a column contains personally identifiable information (PII), it can be locked down even if the user has access to the rest of the data.

Hierarchical Security

For organizations where managers need access to data across multiple business units, **hierarchical security** is key. This model grants managers access to their subordinates' data, even if those subordinates belong to different units or regions.

Types of Hierarchical Security

- **Manager Hierarchy:** A strict, organization-based hierarchy
- **Positional Hierarchy:** A more flexible model based on job positions, allowing for multiple people in a position

Only one type of hierarchy can be applied at a time, so architects must carefully choose the one that best suits the business structure.

Audit

Dataverse also supports **auditing**, allowing organizations to track changes to data, ensuring compliance and providing a transparent way to review actions. This can help not only monitor system usage but also assist in troubleshooting and improving user workflows.

Strategies for Defining Security Roles

There are three main strategies for designing security roles:

1. **Position-Specific:** A role that covers all privileges needed for a specific job function (e.g., Salesperson)

2. **Baseline + Position:** A combination of a baseline role (common privileges) plus additional privileges for specific roles

3. **Baseline + Capability:** A baseline role with additional privileges tailored to specific capabilities (e.g., mobile access)

Security in Apps: A Solution Architect's Perspective

In this chapter, we'll delve into the different layers of security within apps, from the platform to the app level, ensuring you're equipped with the knowledge to make informed decisions when designing secure and efficient solutions.

App-Level Security

The first layer of security is at the app level. Here, you restrict access to the app itself, ensuring that only authorized users can even access the application. This is your first line of defense and prevents unauthorized users from viewing or interacting with sensitive data or processes within the app.

Form-Level Security

For model-driven apps, security can be further refined with form-level controls. This level allows you to restrict access to specific forms based on a user's security group. You can define which forms certain users can access, ensuring that the data they interact with aligns with their job role. By doing so, you maintain control over how users view or input data.

Row-Level Security

At the row level, the Dataverse security model controls access to specific rows of data. This enables fine-grained access management, ensuring that users can only see or modify data that they are authorized to interact with. Whether it's based on ownership, roles, or any other logic you define, row-level security ensures that only the appropriate data is exposed to the user.

Column-Level Security

Lastly, column-level security controls access to individual columns within a table. This allows you to hide or expose specific data fields, ensuring that sensitive information is only accessible to authorized users. It's an important security feature when dealing with tables that contain a mix of public and private data.

Security at the Platform Level

It's important to note that security should primarily be handled at the platform layer, not just within the app layer. While there are ways to limit access through UI customizations (e.g., read-only columns, JavaScript-based masking), these are not true security measures. Users could still access the data through features like Advanced Find or Edit in Excel Online. For proper security, always rely on Dataverse's built-in security features.

Additionally, be mindful that all users are entitled to use the API. Whether it's through partner or community tools, users can potentially access the data using various methods. Ensuring security at the platform level protects data and helps prevent unauthorized access.

Elevated Privileges and Impersonation

As a solution architect, it's vital to avoid assigning high-level privileges to users unnecessarily. In some scenarios, you may need to run plug-ins, classic workflows, or Power Automate flows with elevated privileges to perform actions on behalf of the user. Similarly, API code can impersonate another user if needed. Always consider the implications of such access and use it sparingly.

Automation of Security Management

Automation plays a crucial role in managing users and security settings efficiently. Through APIs, you can automate tasks like creating teams or sharing rows of data. For example, you could automatically elevate the backup account manager's privileges or share data with them when the primary manager is unavailable. This not only streamlines security management but also ensures that security policies are consistently enforced.

Performance Considerations

When designing security for large applications with many users or large amounts of data, performance must be a consideration. Certain practices, such as excessive sharing, using too many business units, or triggering too many processes on events, can cause significant overhead and degrade performance. A poorly designed security model can have the same effect.

Some key techniques to improve performance while maintaining security include

- **Minimizing Sharing:** Whenever possible, share access with teams instead of individual users. This reduces the complexity of security configurations.

- **Consolidating Business Units:** Having too many business units can slow down access, so aim for simplicity.

- **Using Access Teams:** Access teams are more efficient than owner teams, especially for large applications.

- **Testing with Real Scenarios:** Always test security configurations with real-world data and user scenarios to ensure that your design performs well.

Optimizing Usage Patterns

Solution architects should design security to cater to different usage patterns. Users across different departments might require varying access to the same data. The security model should be flexible enough to provide access as needed, without compromising performance or security. The goal is to create a seamless user experience while maintaining strict access control.

Modeling Business Areas Differently

A one-size-fits-all approach doesn't always work when designing security. Different business areas might require different access patterns, and the solution architect should account for this by modeling each area according to its specific needs. This enables you to strike a balance between usability and security.

Model Exceptions As Exceptions

While it's best to design for common access patterns, exceptions may arise. In these cases, it's important to handle these exceptions efficiently. For example, sharing data should be done primarily with teams, as this simplifies access control and keeps things manageable.

Separate Historical from Active Data

For large datasets, you should consider separating historical data from actively used data. This can help optimize performance and simplify security management. In some cases, historical data can be partitioned into separate tables, with a secondary mechanism provided for accessing it when necessary.

Data Model Review for Security

When planning security, it's essential to review the data model to ensure that the design supports secure access. For instance, instead of applying access control directly to Account records, you could move sensitive financial data to a separate table. This allows everyone to access the Account records while keeping the financial data restricted to managers.

Conclusion

By combining the capabilities of Microsoft Copilot, RPA, and robust data modeling and security practices, organizations can drive innovation and efficiency like never before. Copilot and RPA streamline tasks and bring intelligence to workflows, while strong data modeling and security provide the backbone for scalable and compliant solutions. As you apply these concepts, you'll unlock the full potential of the Power Platform to meet business challenges head-on and deliver transformative value.

CHAPTER 5

Implementing Analytics, AI, and ALM Strategies for Power Platform Success

Chapter Goal: To provide readers with the knowledge to assess and implement analytics, AI, and integration strategies while mastering Application Lifecycle Management (ALM) and go-live strategies for Power Platform projects. By the end of this chapter, readers will be equipped to harness data-driven insights, incorporate AI capabilities, integrate systems seamlessly, and manage the end-to-end lifecycle of applications, ensuring successful deployments.

CHAPTER 5   IMPLEMENTING ANALYTICS, AI, AND ALM STRATEGIES FOR
              POWER PLATFORM SUCCESS

Sub-topics:

1. Assessing and Implementing Analytics, AI, and Integration Strategies in Power Platform

2. Application Lifecycle Management and Go-Live Strategies

Assessing and Implementing Analytics, AI, and Integration Strategies, ALM in Power Platform

Introduction

The Power Platform offers immense potential for data-driven decision-making, AI-powered insights, and seamless integration with business systems. Implementing analytics allows organizations to derive actionable insights, while AI capabilities enhance automation and customer engagement. Integration strategies ensure that the platform works cohesively with other systems to streamline operations and foster connectivity.

Equally important is Application Lifecycle Management (ALM), which provides a framework for developing, testing, deploying, and maintaining applications effectively. Combined with strategic go-live planning, ALM ensures that solutions are delivered with minimal disruption and maximum impact.

In this chapter, we will explore how to assess analytics and AI requirements, implement integration strategies, and design effective ALM processes. We'll also cover essential go-live strategies, ensuring that your Power Platform applications are deployed seamlessly and optimized for long-term success.

Analytics and Reporting

Introduction

Reporting and analytics are integral parts of any solution built on Microsoft Power Platform. Whether you are working on the sales, development, or deployment stages, understanding how to incorporate these features is essential. A solution architect must design solutions that not only provide insights into existing data but also anticipate future needs through proactive reporting and AI-driven insights.

The solution architect's role is to evaluate different reporting approaches based on the requirements of the project, ensuring the data model and integration strategies align with the analytics needs of the business. Furthermore, AI technologies can enhance business solutions by providing intelligent insights, predictions, and recommendations that drive business actions.

The Solution Architect's Role in Reporting and Analytics

Throughout the lifecycle of a project, reporting and analytics are considered at each phase:

1. **Sales and Presales:** In these early stages, the solution architect uses reporting to impress the customer, demonstrating the value of the proposed solution through data-driven insights.

2. **Analyze Phase:** During the Analyze phase, the solution architect clarifies the actual reporting and analytics goals based on customer needs, ensuring that the solution will fulfill these requirements.

3. **Design Phase:** In this phase, the architect ensures that the data model incorporates the necessary data structures and relationships to support reporting and analytics capabilities. The architect must consider how the data will be stored, queried, and visualized.

4. **Deploy Stage:** At deployment, self-service reporting is set up, and users are trained to take advantage of the reporting capabilities.

Solution architects must ensure that the data model not only supports application processing but also meets the reporting and analytics needs, often involving both operational and advanced reporting capabilities.

Types of Reporting and Analytics

Solution architects must evaluate different categories of reporting and analytics, each of which serves distinct purposes within the business solution.

1. Operational Reporting

Operational reporting typically uses data stored in **Microsoft Dataverse**, providing insights in real time or near real time. These reports are used within Power Apps to present relevant data to the user as they interact with the app. The focus is on daily operations and transaction-based insights.

- **Use Case:** Displaying sales performance data, customer service requests, or inventory levels in a Power App

2. Self-Service BI

Self-service Business Intelligence (BI) allows users to access and analyze data independently without requiring extensive technical expertise. This often involves extracting data from Dataverse, refreshing it on a schedule, and then analyzing it within tools like **Power BI**.

- **Use Case:** A business user generating their own reports on customer engagement or product performance from the data stored in Dataverse

3. Enterprise BI

Enterprise BI integrates data from multiple sources, including external systems, for comprehensive reporting and analytics. These reports are often used at an organizational level and can be visualized through enterprise tools such as **Power BI**.

- **Use Case:** Consolidated reports integrating data from Dataverse, external databases, and Excel for company-wide decision-making

Prebuilt Insights in Microsoft Dynamics 365

Microsoft Dynamics 365 apps offer extensive prebuilt insights, which solution architects can leverage to fulfill reporting requirements without the need for custom development. These insights provide businesses with intelligent analysis and actionable recommendations out of the box.

- **Dynamics 365 Sales Insights:** Provides insights into sales performance, including forecasting and lead scoring

- **Dynamics 365 Customer Insights - Data:** Helps businesses understand their customers better through data aggregation and segmentation

- **Dynamics 365 Fraud Protection:** Analyzes transaction data to identify and prevent fraud

These prebuilt insights can be integrated into the solution, reducing the need for custom reporting and enabling rapid deployment.

Additionally, **Microsoft Power BI template apps** for Dynamics 365 are available for specific business processes and can be deployed directly to meet reporting requirements.

Key Questions for Solution Architects

When evaluating reporting and analytics requirements for a solution, solution architects should consider several key questions to ensure the solution meets business needs:

1. **What data is required?** Understand which data sources are necessary to create the reports and ensure it is available.

2. **Is external data required?** Identify if data from external systems (e.g., third-party applications or databases) is needed for the report.

3. **Does the requirement fit with prebuilt insights?** Determine if Dynamics 365 prebuilt insights or Power BI template apps can satisfy the reporting need.

4. **Who consumes the report/visualization, and are they existing users?** Understand the target audience for the reports and whether they are already using the solution or need additional access.

5. **How fresh does the data need to be?** Establish whether the data should be real time, near real time, or if it can be historical or batch processed.

6. **Should something be built, or can an existing report/view satisfy the requirement?** Evaluate if a custom report is necessary, or if an existing report/view can fulfill the need.

7. **What is the expected action after reviewing the report?** Determine the actions users need to take after consuming the report and whether it can be automated.

8. **Can the actions be predicted or automated?** Look for opportunities to use AI-driven insights to predict actions or automate business processes based on data analysis.

Leveraging AI for Reporting and Analytics

AI plays an increasingly important role in enhancing reporting and analytics by delivering proactive insights and automating decision-making. Solution architects should explore AI capabilities, such as

- **Power BI AI Insights:** Leverage built-in machine learning models to gain insights, detect patterns, and make predictions based on historical data.

- **Power Automate AI Builder:** Use AI to automate tasks such as document processing, form recognition, and data categorization.

- **Predictive Analytics:** Use historical data and machine learning algorithms to forecast future trends and outcomes.

By incorporating AI into the solution, solution architects can deliver more powerful, data-driven insights that not only help businesses understand what is happening now but also predict and optimize future outcomes.

Power Platform Reporting Capabilities

Microsoft Power Platform provides several reporting options to meet a wide variety of business needs. These reporting options can be used in conjunction with Microsoft Dataverse, which stores and manages the data for Power Apps, Power Automate, and Power Virtual Agents. By integrating reporting and analytics into the platform, solution architects can ensure that business users have access to the insights they need for decision-making.

1. Model-Driven Apps

Dataverse offers several built-in reporting tools for model-driven apps, each catering to different types of reporting needs.

- **Views:** Views are predefined queries on the data stored in Dataverse. They allow users to display selected columns with filters applied. Views can be used for simple reporting needs, such as creating lists or tables of data.

- **Charts:** Charts visualize the data that is displayed in a view. They help present data in graphical formats, such as bar, pie, or line charts, making it easier to analyze trends or distributions.

- **Dashboards:** Dashboards are collections of views and charts that provide an overview of data. They can be interactive, allowing users to filter data, take actions, and drill down for more detailed insights. Power BI visualizations can also be embedded into dashboards to enhance reporting.

Advantages of Dataverse Reporting Options

- **Simple Access from Within Apps:** Users can access reports without leaving the app, offering a seamless experience.

- **Always Up to Date:** Data displayed in views, charts, and dashboards is always current, ensuring users are working with the latest information.

- **Security Model Enforcement:** Security roles and permissions applied in Dataverse extend to reports, ensuring data access is controlled appropriately.

- **Included in Solution Packages:** Reporting tools are part of solution packages, making it easier to deploy across environments.

- **User-Friendly:** No special technical skills are required to create views, charts, and dashboards, allowing business users to create personal reports.

Disadvantages of Dataverse Reporting Options

- **Limited Visualizations:** The visualizations in views and charts are relatively simple compared to more advanced reporting tools.

- **Limited Data Scope:** Data in views is limited to a single table or related tables in many-to-one relationships, restricting more complex cross-table reporting.

- **Real-Time Data:** Data is always current and cannot be "frozen" at a specific point in time for historical analysis.

- **Limited to 50,000 Rows:** Charts and dashboards are restricted to a maximum of 50,000 rows of data, and views only display the first 5,000 rows.

2. Export to Excel

Dataverse offers the ability to export data to Excel, either as static data or through a dynamic query.

- **Static Data:** This option allows users to export a snapshot of the data at a particular point in time, which is useful when sharing data externally or with users who are not app users.

- **Dynamic Query:** Users can export data with dynamic queries, allowing for real-time data to be pulled into Excel. Dynamic queries enable users to refresh their data directly within Excel, ensuring the report remains up to date with the Dataverse data.

Exported data can be used to analyze the information further, especially when users require the flexibility of Excel's advanced functions, like PivotTables and charts.

3. Word and Excel Templates

Word and Excel templates can be used for reporting purposes. These templates can generate formatted reports based on data in Dataverse:

- **Word Templates:** Useful for generating reports based on a single row and its related rows (e.g., generating a customer report with their related orders).

- **Excel Templates:** Useful for exporting a list of rows or a view of data to Excel, where additional analysis or visualizations can be created. Excel templates can include built-in charts and graphs for deeper insights.

> **Note** Word and Excel templates can't be included in a solution package and can only be used within the environment they were created in.

4. Report Wizard

The Report Wizard in model-driven apps is a tool that simplifies the process of creating SQL Server Reporting Services (SSRS) reports. Users can generate tabular reports or reports with charts. These reports can be downloaded and edited for customization, and they can be included in solution packages for deployment.

> **Note** Reports created through the Report Wizard are basic in layout but can be edited and customized further.

5. SQL Server Reporting Services (SSRS)

For more complex reporting needs, data analysts can use **SQL Server Reporting Services** (SSRS) and **Visual Studio** to create detailed reports that can pull data from multiple sources. These reports can aggregate large datasets and allow for more sophisticated data analysis.

Important Consideration: SSRS reports run on a timer, with a maximum execution time of five minutes. Reports that require more time to process will time out, which can be mitigated by optimizing queries and limiting the number of records processed.

Tips for Creating Reports

- **Limit Query Results:** Use filters to limit the data being queried (e.g., by time period or specific fields).

- **Limit the Number of Tables:** Reduce the number of tables involved in queries to speed up processing time.

- **Use Aggregation in the Database:** For summarized reports, push aggregation to the database rather than fetching raw data and performing aggregation in SSRS.

Alternative Reporting Options

1. Advanced Find

Advanced Find is an invaluable tool for creating ad hoc queries. It allows users to define custom queries, save them as personal views, and use these queries for other reporting functions like

- Exporting to Excel
- Creating Excel templates
- Generating bulk deletes
- Creating dashboards

For quick, impromptu reporting, combining **Advanced Find** with **Excel** is an excellent option for users who need to create a report without a full-scale development process.

2. Power BI

Power BI should always be considered for reporting and analytics. It provides advanced visualization capabilities, including interactive dashboards, and can integrate data from Dataverse, external systems, and other data sources. Power BI allows for deeper analysis and rich visualizations compared to the built-in Dataverse tools.

When to use Power BI:

- For complex, enterprise-level reporting needs that require advanced visualizations and interactivity

- To combine multiple data sources (internal and external)

- For scenarios that require predictive analytics or AI-driven insights

Artificial Intelligence

AI (Artificial Intelligence) is a field of computer science aimed at creating machines that simulate human behavior. The technology involves learning from the environment, reasoning, knowledge representation, and abstract thinking. Machine learning, a subset of AI, focuses on enabling machines to learn autonomously from data, making it the backbone of modern AI applications.

Microsoft provides a range of AI and machine learning services to enhance data functionality:

Dynamics 365 AI Apps

Solution architects should be aware of the following prebuilt insights offered by Dynamics 365 apps:

- **Dynamics 365 Sales Insights:** Provides AI-driven insights for sales teams

- **Dynamics 365 Customer Insights:** Uses data to generate customer-centric insights

- **Dynamics 365 Fraud Protection:** Helps to detect and prevent fraudulent activity

Azure Cognitive Services

Azure Cognitive Services is a suite of prebuilt AI services that can be easily integrated into applications without needing in-depth expertise in machine learning. It offers APIs for

- **Computer Vision:** For analyzing and understanding images

- **Natural Language Processing:** For understanding and processing human language

- **Speech:** For speech recognition and synthesis

- **Decision:** To help make automated decisions based on data

OpenAI Integration

Cognitive Services also includes access to **OpenAI**, which can be integrated via REST APIs for various AI-driven solutions.

Azure Machine Learning

Azure Machine Learning provides a more customizable environment for building machine learning models; it is useful when Cognitive Services or AI Builder doesn't meet the requirements. It supports a wide range of tools, languages, and frameworks.

AI Builder

AI Builder is a tool within Microsoft Power Platform that enables users to build AI models without needing coding or machine learning expertise. It provides several prebuilt models, including

- **Invoice Processing:** Automates invoice data extraction
- **Text Recognition:** Extracts text from images and documents
- **Sentiment Analysis:** Detects emotional tone in text
- **Language Detection:** Identifies the language of a text
- **Business Card Reader:** Extracts data from business cards

Integration with Power Platform

AI Builder can be used with **Canvas Apps** and **Power Automate** to automate workflows or enhance user input:

- **Canvas Apps:** Integrate AI models to process images, text, or data directly within the app.
- **Power Automate:** Trigger flows based on events like record creation or image storage, using AI Builder models for data categorization, predictions, and text processing.

Choosing the Right AI Solution

Solution architects must decide on the appropriate AI solution, such as whether to use

- **AI Builder** for simpler applications
- **Cognitive Services** for more advanced, prebuilt models
- **Azure Machine Learning** for custom-built, enterprise-level machine learning models

Integration in Power Platform: The Solution Architect's Role

As a solution architect, one of your core responsibilities is to guide and lead the identification and implementation of integrations within Microsoft Power Platform. Integration, in this context, is about connecting different systems or components to create a unified and seamless user experience. The goal is to ensure that different systems and applications within the broader architecture work together effectively, enabling greater efficiency and consistency in processes.

In this chapter, we'll explore the concept of integration and the solution architect's role in designing and implementing integrations within the Power Platform ecosystem.

What Is Integration?

Integration refers to the process of connecting disparate systems, applications, or data sources to create a unified system that behaves as one entity. This is crucial because systems that operate independently may lead to inefficiencies, errors, or fragmented user experiences. Integration is akin to stitching together separate pieces to form a cohesive whole.

A well-integrated system ensures

- **Data Integrity:** Consistent and accurate data is shared across systems.

- **Better User Adoption:** A seamless user experience across applications leads to greater acceptance.

- **Higher ROI:** Efficiency gains and reduced redundancies improve overall return on investment.

Consider the business app you're building as a component in a larger enterprise process that spans across multiple systems. Your app might need to connect to these systems to deliver value, and integration is what makes this possible.

Why Is Integration Necessary?

Integration is necessary for several key reasons, often arising from specific challenges within the enterprise. Here are six common factors that make integration indispensable:

1. **Usability:** Users often interact with multiple systems to perform a task, leading to inefficiencies. Integration simplifies this by providing a unified interface, reducing training costs and increasing consistency in user experiences.

2. **Volume:** When data volumes are large or regularly updated, duplicating data across systems can be inefficient and costly. Instead of copying or migrating data, integration enables access to centralized data in real time.

3. **Real-Time Access:** In many cases, businesses need up-to-date customer information, often stored in different systems. Integration enables real-time access to this data, ensuring that decisions are based on the most current information available.

4. **Cost:** Some functionality, like address lookup, may be cheaper when accessed externally rather than recreating the same capabilities internally. Integration can reduce costs by tapping into existing third-party services.

5. **Duplication:** Data consistency is critical for processes like service resource allocation. Without integration, there could be duplication or inconsistencies that result in operational failures, like double-booking. Integration ensures that critical data, like resource allocation, is consistent across all systems.

6. **Reuse:** Reimplementing common functionality in multiple systems can be costly, especially considering maintenance and testing. Integration allows organizations to reuse existing capabilities, promoting consistency and reducing overhead costs.

Types of Integration

Integration can be broadly classified into three types:

1. **Data Integration:** Combines data from different sources and presents a unified view to the user, often in the form of a consolidated dashboard or report

2. **Application Integration:** Focuses on connecting applications at a higher level, facilitating communication between apps to streamline business processes

3. **Process Integration:** Involves combining multiple systems, each of which contributes to a specific part of a larger business process, ensuring that the overall process runs smoothly

A well-rounded Power Platform solution might require a mix of these integration types to achieve the desired results.

How Solution Architects Help with Integration

Solution architects play a pivotal role in the integration process. Their expertise is critical in the following ways:

1. **Identify Integration Requirements:** The first step is to assess the systems and processes that need to be integrated. This involves understanding the business needs and determining how the Power Platform can best fit into the broader enterprise architecture.

2. **Lead the Integration Design:** Once the requirements are identified, the solution architect leads the design of how these integrations will be implemented. This involves defining the architecture and ensuring that the integration aligns with the overall solution's goals.

3. **Evaluate Integration Tools:** Solution architects are responsible for evaluating third-party integration tools or services. The right tools ensure that integrations are efficient and fit within the broader architecture.

4. **Ensure Robust and Scalable Integrations:** While integrating systems, it's crucial that the integrations do not compromise the stability or scalability of the solution. A solution architect ensures that integrations are built to handle future growth and remain resilient to changes.

5. **Disaster Recovery Planning:** Integration design should also consider disaster recovery plans to ensure that in the event of a failure, the system can recover quickly without losing data or functionality.

6. **Evaluate the Cost of Doing Nothing:** The solution architect must always assess the cost of inaction before moving forward with integration. This involves understanding the cost of solving the problem manually or through inefficient processes and determining whether integration provides a better solution in the long run. For instance, if an integration takes six months to develop but only synchronizes a small amount of data, is the benefit worth the time and effort?

Integration Challenges in Power Platform: Overcoming the Hurdles

Integrating systems, data, and processes across different platforms can be a complex, expensive, and challenging task. As a solution architect, you must navigate these challenges to ensure a smooth and resilient integration process. In this section, we will explore the common challenges, factors influencing integration design, causes of failure, and strategies for resilience.

Common Integration Challenges

Integrations often present challenges that can hinder the effectiveness of the solution. Some of the common challenges include

- **Complexity of Integration:** Integrating systems with different architectures, technologies, or standards can be challenging, leading to delays, cost overruns, and technical issues.

- **Brittleness of Integrations:** Without proper design, integrations can be fragile, making it difficult to make future changes or scale the system.

- **Quality of Data:** Poor-quality or inconsistent data can complicate integrations, leading to errors and unreliable outputs.

- **Latency and Reliability:** Long delays in data processing or communication between systems can result in inefficiencies, while low reliability can impact business operations.

- **Security and Compliance:** Meeting security requirements and ensuring data compliance can be complex, especially when dealing with sensitive or regulated data.

The solution architect's role is to address these challenges, ensuring that integrations are well-designed, maintainable, and scalable.

Influencers of Integration Design

Several factors influence how you design and implement integrations in Power Platform. These include

1. **Volume of Data:** The amount of data being moved or accessed can impact the choice of integration tools and methods. High data volumes may require batch processing or more powerful integration tools.

2. **Quality of Data:** Poor-quality data, such as duplicates or incomplete information, can undermine the success of the integration. Ensuring data integrity is crucial for a smooth integration process.

3. **Latency:** The time it takes to access or process data from external systems can affect user experience and system performance. Integrations should be designed to handle latency effectively.

4. **Security Requirements:** Data security and privacy are essential considerations, particularly when dealing with personal or sensitive data. Integration solutions should meet these requirements to mitigate risks.

5. **Reliability:** Ensuring high availability and reliability of integrated systems is crucial to maintain continuous operations and minimize downtime.

6. **Impact of Data Duplication:** Duplication of data or functionality across systems can lead to inconsistencies and errors. Integrating systems effectively helps to avoid this problem.

7. **Cost, Time, and Resources:** The resources required to implement an integration—whether in terms of time, cost, or personnel—will influence the choice of solution. Balancing these factors is essential.

8. **Internal Politics:** Organizational dynamics and competing priorities can sometimes impact the design and implementation of integrations. Navigating these internal factors is a part of the solution architect's role.

Causes of Integration Failures

Several factors can contribute to the failure of integrations. Identifying these factors early in the design process can help you avoid costly mistakes:

1. **Underestimating Complexity:** The complexity of integrating different systems can be easily underestimated, leading to unforeseen challenges down the line.

2. **Poor User Experience:** If the integrated solution provides a poor user experience, it can lead to low adoption and hinder the effectiveness of the integration.

CHAPTER 5   IMPLEMENTING ANALYTICS, AI, AND ALM STRATEGIES FOR POWER PLATFORM SUCCESS

3. **Fragile Systems:** Increasing the cohesion of components without proper planning can create fragile systems that are difficult to change or scale.

4. **Lack of Knowledge:** A lack of understanding of what Microsoft Power Platform or other systems can and cannot do can lead to poorly designed integrations.

5. **Poor Data Quality:** Integrating systems with poor or dirty data can result in errors, inaccuracies, and business inefficiencies.

6. **Unclear System of Record:** Without a clear definition of the system of record, it can be difficult to determine which system holds the "true" version of the data, leading to data inconsistencies.

7. **Lack of Coordination:** Integrating systems involves multiple parties. Lack of coordination between these parties can lead to missed requirements and implementation issues.

8. **Unfamiliarity with Power Platform:** If the parties involved in building the integrations are unfamiliar with Microsoft Power Platform, it can lead to suboptimal solutions.

Designing for Resilience

As a solution architect, you must design integrations that are resilient and can withstand failures. This involves considering potential points of failure and ensuring that your integrations can recover gracefully.

Here are some strategies to design resilient integrations:

1. **Expect Transient Errors:** Transient errors, such as temporary network failures, are common in integrations. These errors should be anticipated and handled appropriately.

2. **Escalating Retry Logic:** Implementing retry logic with a circuit breaker pattern ensures that if an integration fails, it will attempt to retry. After a certain number of retries, the system should fail gracefully, alerting the team to address the issue.

3. **Use Loosely Coupled Techniques:** Using techniques like queuing and event-driven architectures increases the resiliency of the integration by decoupling systems and allowing them to operate independently.

4. **Handle Common Failures:** Anticipate and include handling for common failures in your design, such as network interruptions, data validation issues, or system downtimes.

The Integration Design Process

Integration is rarely a one-size-fits-all process. Each project presents unique challenges that require customized solutions. The integration design process typically follows these steps:

1. **Identify Integration Requirements:** Understand the business goals and technical needs of the integration. This will guide your decisions on the type of integration needed.

2. **Evaluate Integration Scenarios:** Based on the requirements, evaluate potential integration scenarios and tools. Consider the strengths and weaknesses of Microsoft Power Platform and other systems involved.

3. **Design and Develop Integrations:** Once the integration approach is defined, begin designing and developing the solution. Ensure that it fits within the overall architecture and meets the business and technical needs.

4. **Test and Validate:** Testing is a critical step in the integration process. Validate the integration's functionality, performance, and security to ensure it meets the defined requirements.

5. **Monitor and Optimize:** Once the integration is live, continuously monitor its performance and optimize as necessary to address issues such as latency, data quality, or user experience.

Categorizing Data for Integration

When evaluating data for integration, solution architects should categorize data based on various factors to determine the best approach for integration. These categories include

- **Volatility:** How rapidly the data is changing. Highly volatile data may require more frequent synchronization or real-time integration.

- **Volume:** The size of the data being integrated. High volumes may require batch processing or more powerful tools to handle the data load.

- **Time Sensitivity:** Whether the data needs to be processed in real time or if batch processing is sufficient.

- **Regulated Data:** Data that is subject to legal or compliance restrictions, such as personal data, which may need to be stored or transmitted securely.

- **Licensed Data:** Data that is licensed and subject to usage restrictions. Integration solutions must comply with licensing terms and limitations.

By categorizing the data, you can design the most appropriate integration strategy and avoid costly mistakes.

Application Lifecycle Management and Go-Live Strategies

Introduction

The application lifecycle is a continuous and iterative process that encompasses planning, tracking, developing, building, testing, deploying, operating, monitoring, and learning from discovery. This lifecycle ensures that applications evolve and improve over time, meeting user needs while adapting to changes in the business environment.

In this module, we'll explore how to define and structure your environment, compose solutions, and develop a robust ALM strategy for Microsoft Power Platform. You will also learn how to leverage Azure DevOps and its build and release pipelines to implement efficient ALM processes.

CHAPTER 5　IMPLEMENTING ANALYTICS, AI, AND ALM STRATEGIES FOR POWER PLATFORM SUCCESS

Application Lifecycle Management with Microsoft Power Platform

Microsoft Power Platform leverages **solutions** as the primary mechanism for Application Lifecycle Management (ALM). Solutions enable you to package apps, customizations, and components such as site maps, entities, fields, charts, and plug-ins. These solutions can be exported from one environment and imported into another, making it easy to move components across environments like development, testing, and production.

The process of ALM with Microsoft Power Platform involves packaging components into **solutions** and using **Dataverse** as the central repository to store all artifacts. Solutions are then exported and imported through Azure DevOps, facilitating a streamlined development-to-deployment workflow. Microsoft's approach to ALM provides tools to support the export and import of solutions, enabling automated release management and simplifying the deployment process.

Microsoft's Vision for ALM

Microsoft envisions an ALM process that makes it easier for app builders to manage their environments and deploy applications through automated, repeatable processes. The key pillars of Microsoft Power Platform's ALM vision are

- **Quick Start:** Enabling app builders to quickly set up environments with the latest builds, connect to source control, and start making changes
- **Build:** Simplifying the tooling and speeding up development cycles for efficient app creation

- **Deploy:** Supporting an automated and predictable deployment methodology for all environments

- **Manage:** Providing greater flexibility for app builders to manage and dispose of preconfigured environments as needed

- **Monitor:** Incorporating telemetry and feedback loops to monitor applications post-deployment, ensuring continuous improvement

As the Microsoft Power Platform ecosystem continues to evolve, it is essential for solution architects to stay aligned with these developments. Understanding the vision for ALM is crucial for crafting your strategy and using the platform's capabilities to optimize the development and deployment process.

The Solution Architect's Role in ALM

Solution architects play a key role in defining and executing the ALM strategy for Power Platform projects. They must lead the establishment of a clear ALM plan that supports the journey from development to production. Their responsibilities include

- **Leading the ALM Plan:** Designing and implementing the overall ALM plan, ensuring it aligns with the project's goals and requirements

- **Evaluating ALM Complexity:** Determining the level of sophistication needed for the ALM process based on project scope and complexity

- **Collaborating with Teams:** Working closely with development, testing, and operations teams to ensure smooth implementation of the ALM plan

CHAPTER 5 IMPLEMENTING ANALYTICS, AI, AND ALM STRATEGIES FOR POWER PLATFORM SUCCESS

Solutions in Microsoft Power Platform

In the context of Microsoft Power Platform, **solutions** are essential containers that track and manage customizations in a Dataverse environment. These solutions allow the transport of apps, custom components, and configurations from one environment to another, enabling organizations to apply and distribute customizations seamlessly across different stages of development and deployment.

Key Characteristics of Solutions

Solutions consist of

- **Metadata and Configuration Data:** Solutions do not contain actual business data, but they include metadata like tables, forms, views, processes, and business rules.

- **Multiple Components:** These components can range from model-driven apps, Canvas apps, flows, custom connectors, scripts, to web resources and more.

- **Packaged Units:** Solutions are packaged for export and import between environments or checked into source control as source code for asset management.

Solutions play a pivotal role in ALM by providing a mechanism to manage and distribute app customizations across different environments.

Types of Solutions

1. **Unmanaged Solutions**

    - Used in development environments.

    - Suitable for when configuration changes are being made and are to be transported to other development environments.

    - These solutions are checked into source control and should be treated as your source of truth.

2. **Managed Solutions**

    - Used for distributing solutions to non-development environments such as testing, UAT, SIT, and production.

    - Managed solutions can be serviced (upgraded, patched, deleted) independently, making them an essential aspect of deployment.

    - ALM best practices suggest that managed solutions should be generated by a build server and considered a build artifact.

Solution Layering

Solution layering refers to the dependency structure that is built when one solution extends or customizes a component introduced by another solution. This layering impacts how solutions interact within Dataverse:

- **Unmanaged Layer:** Houses all imported unmanaged solutions and customizations. All unmanaged solutions share a single unmanaged layer.

- **Managed Layer:** Contains all managed solutions and the system solution. When multiple managed solutions are installed, the last one installed takes precedence in case of conflicts, applying a "Last one wins" approach or using merge logic.

Understanding solution layering is essential for managing dependencies and determining how changes in one solution may affect another.

Strategies for Solution Structure

When planning your solution structure, there are several strategies that vary in complexity:

- **Single Solution:** The simplest approach, where all customizations are grouped into a single solution. This is effective for smaller projects with minimal dependencies.

- **Multiple Solutions:** For larger projects, you may use multiple solutions to keep things organized and modular. However, this increases complexity and requires careful management of dependencies.

- **Multiple Solutions with Shared Components:** Solutions can share components when they are compatible, and these shared components must use the same solution publisher to be installed together.

Rules for Creating Solutions

- **Solution Publisher:** Always create and use a solution publisher to ensure consistency across all solutions.

- **Keep the Solution Structure Simple:** Overcomplicating solutions can lead to difficulties in tracking and managing them.

- **Segment the Solution:** Add only the necessary components to a solution, ensuring that only the required subcomponents are included.

Solution Splitting: Horizontal and Vertical Approaches

Horizontal Solution Splitting: This approach creates solutions that contain only components of the same type, simplifying the structure, for example, a solution for only tables or only apps.

Vertical Solution Layering: This involves grouping components based on functional areas. Often, a shared base solution contains common tables and processes, while separate solutions are created for each key business area (e.g., sales, HR, finance).

Combining Horizontal and Vertical Approaches: In larger environments, combining both splitting techniques allows for a more organized structure, with a base solution for common components and additional solutions for different business areas or app functionalities.

Best Practices for Solutions

1. **Use Multiple Solutions with Purpose:** While you may be tempted to use multiple solutions, this should be done only when there is a clear purpose, as it adds complexity.

2. **Avoid Multiple Solutions with Shared Components:** When solutions share components, managing dependencies becomes challenging.

3. **Manage Dependencies Carefully:** Ensure that dependencies between solutions are tracked and maintained effectively.

4. **Design Solutions to Minimize Interference:** Avoid conflicts between components by segmenting solutions logically.

ALM with Azure DevOps for Microsoft Power Platform

Application Lifecycle Management (ALM) with **Azure DevOps** plays a crucial role in managing the development, testing, and deployment of solutions, ensuring streamlined processes and minimizing errors. Solution architects define the stages through which changes move (e.g., **dev ➤ test ➤ production**) and the methods of promotion—whether manual or automated. Azure DevOps is designed to support this process by using **Continuous Integration (CI)** and **Continuous Deployment (CD)** pipelines to automate and manage deployments across environments.

Key Components of Azure DevOps

Azure DevOps is a suite of services that helps development teams plan, collaborate, and manage code development and deployment processes. Key components include

1. **Azure Boards:** For tracking work, planning tasks, and collaborating on development efforts

2. **Azure Pipelines:** Automates CI/CD for building, testing, and deploying solutions across environments

3. **Azure Repos:** Provides source control to track changes in code

4. **Azure Test Plans:** Manages and tracks scripted tests for applications

5. **Azure Artifacts:** Publishes solutions built by pipelines to be used across environments

Pipelines in Power Platform

Azure Pipelines play a crucial role in automating the build and deployment process for Microsoft Power Platform solutions.

Build Pipelines

They are used to automate tasks like

- **Creating development environments**
- **Committing changes** to source control
- **Running the Solution Checker** to ensure quality
- **Performing automated testing**
- **Building output solutions** (managed or unmanaged)

Release Pipelines

They are used to

- **Deploy solutions** to test or production environments
- **Automate testing** as part of the release process
- **Pause for approvals** before advancing to the next stage (e.g., UAT or production)

Tasks in Microsoft Power Platform Build Tools can integrate with other Azure DevOps tasks to form comprehensive build and release pipelines. Typical pipeline stages include

1. **Initiate:** Setting up the environment and initial configurations
2. **Export from Dev:** Extracting solutions from the development environment
3. **Build:** Running the solution through a build process
4. **Release:** Deploying the solution to staging, testing, or production environments

Deployment Methodologies in Azure DevOps

When setting up release pipelines, you must decide on how to trigger the deployment. There are several deployment methodologies:

1. **Manual Triggers**
    - Often used for **immediate fixes** or **patches**.
    - A user manually triggers the release pipeline, providing quick deployment in urgent situations (e.g., bug fixes in UAT).

2. **Scheduled Triggers**

   - Used for regular deployment cycles (e.g., weekly releases).

   - Ideal for development teams with a predefined schedule for builds and releases, as in the case of **Contoso Bank**, where the release pipeline is based on sprint cycles.

3. **Pull Request Triggers**

   - Triggered when a pull request is raised, ensuring that only verified code reaches the production pipeline.

4. **Continuous Deployment**

   - Automatically pushes the latest build to other environments as soon as it's available. This ensures that any new updates are automatically propagated across the pipeline.

Go-Live Plan for Solution Deployment

The go-live phase is critical for the success of any solution. It is essential to complete several activities beforehand to ensure a smooth transition to production. These activities include **performance testing**, **deployment planning**, and **risk assessment**. Each plays a vital role in ensuring the solution performs well under real-world conditions and that deployment is seamless.

CHAPTER 5   IMPLEMENTING ANALYTICS, AI, AND ALM STRATEGIES FOR POWER PLATFORM SUCCESS

1. Performance Testing

Performance testing is crucial to ensure the application can handle daily user loads and business processes efficiently. Without performance testing, users may face delays in loading pages or completing tasks, leading to poor adoption and satisfaction.

Key Considerations for Performance Testing

- **Dedicated Test Environment:** Ensure a dedicated environment is set up for performance testing that mirrors production conditions.

- **Master or Reference Data:** Identify and prepare the required data sets that will be used in testing.

- **Key Business Scenarios:** Define the critical business processes and set baselines to measure performance.

- **Concurrent Load:** Identify the expected number of concurrent users and plan tests for that load, factoring in peak volumes.

- **Latency Testing:** Perform latency tests across various locations where the application will be used to ensure optimal user experience.

- **Data Population:** Ensure that the required data is populated in the testing environment before testing begins.

Solution Architect's Responsibilities

- **Identify Hotspots:** Determine key areas of the application that could potentially cause performance issues and ensure they are tested.

- **Plan for Peak Volume:** Anticipate peak usage scenarios and plan for slightly higher volumes than expected.

- **SLAs Compliance:** Ensure the solution meets contractual performance service-level agreements (SLAs) by validating against these benchmarks.

- **Monitor Network Traffic:** Use tools like **Microsoft Azure Monitor** and **Azure App Insights** to check network latency, bandwidth, and app performance, especially for remote or distributed teams.

Performance testing should be completed well before go-live to identify issues and mitigate risks. The results may necessitate remediation steps and support requests for further optimization.

2. Deployment Planning

Effective deployment planning is crucial to ensure the solution is successfully transitioned to production with minimal disruptions. The deployment plan outlines the activities required to deploy the solution successfully.

Key Aspects of Deployment Planning

- **Environment Setup:** Set up the production and staging environments, including necessary configurations and resources.

- **Testing:** Ensure different types of testing (e.g., functional, integration, UAT) are performed to confirm readiness for production.

- **User Training:** Conduct comprehensive training for end users to ensure they are prepared to use the new solution.

- **Data Migration:** Plan for secure and accurate migration of data to the production environment, including any transformations needed.

- **Rollout Strategy:** Define the steps for phased or full rollout, including any pilot testing or beta phases.

- **Deployment Support:** Ensure a team is in place to support the deployment and handle any issues that arise during or immediately after go-live.

Solution Architect's Responsibilities

- **Ensure Sequence of Events:** Ensure that all steps required for the go-live process are clearly defined and scheduled.

- **Risk Identification:** Continuously assess risks during the deployment process and have contingency plans in place.

- **Deployment Team:** Make sure the necessary resources and support teams are in place, including those for troubleshooting and issue resolution during deployment.

The solution architect may not create the full deployment plan but will typically provide input and ensure the overall approach is solid. They are also often the first point of contact when deployment progress is at risk or a customer expresses concerns.

3. Risk Assessment

The solution architect has the deepest understanding of the system and its capabilities. Therefore, they should conduct a thorough risk assessment to anticipate potential issues before they arise.

Key Questions for Risk Assessment

- **What could break?** Consider areas of the solution that might fail or experience issues.

- **What might not work as designed?** Identify components that might not perform as expected, especially under real-world usage conditions.

- **What if other systems fail?** Assess dependencies on external systems and plan for their failure (e.g., third-party APIs or integrations).

- **Do we have the proper deployment sequence?** Ensure the deployment process is well-organized, with appropriate sequencing of tasks and checkpoints.

The solution architect should always prepare for the worst-case scenario, but they should also ensure that alternative plans are in place to minimize the impact of potential failures. This proactive approach helps the team remain prepared and confident during the go-live phase.

Common Go-Live Problems

Several challenges can occur during go-live that may jeopardize the success of the deployment. These include

1. **No Rollback Plan:** Lack of a contingency plan if the deployment encounters issues, which can create delays or failures.

2. **Incorrect Assumptions:** Misunderstanding about user workstation or network configurations can lead to performance issues or access problems.

3. **Insufficient Real-World Testing:** Customizations may not meet real user needs, or the system may not perform well under a real-world load if sufficient testing was not performed.

Mitigating Go-Live Problems

- **Streamline the Plan:** Look for ways to simplify the deployment process, such as pre-deploying mobile apps or automating configurations.

- **Prioritize Data Migration:** Ensure that critical data is migrated first to avoid delays in production.

- **Access Testing:** Provide users access to a dummy production environment to resolve any access issues before go-live.

- **Parallel System Run:** If feasible, run the old and new systems in parallel and gradually transition users, ensuring that issues are caught early.

Dealing with Problems Post-Go-Live

After go-live, the solution architect is often the first line of support when issues arise. It is important to quickly identify, isolate, and simplify problems.

Problem-Solving Steps

1. **Triage:** Prioritize issues based on business impact and urgency.

2. **Isolation:** Isolate the root cause of the issue, whether it's a configuration error, data problem, or system issue.

3. **Simplification:** Address issues in a way that simplifies the solution, avoiding overcomplicated fixes.

4. **Microsoft Power Platform Tools:** Leverage the built-in features of Power Platform tools, such as troubleshooting capabilities in **Power Apps** and **Power Automate**, to resolve issues efficiently.

Considerations Before Making Changes

- **Immediate Impact:** Consider how the changes will affect the system and users in the short term.

- **Long-Term Impact:** Evaluate the long-term effects of mitigation strategies, including any future updates or maintenance needs.

Summary of Solution Architect's Role in Go-Live

- **Go-Live Readiness Review:** Conduct thorough assessments to ensure the customer is fully prepared.

- **Problem Prevention:** Proactively address potential issues that could cause delays or performance problems.

- **Automate Key Activities:** Use automation to streamline deployment and reduce risk.

- **Post-Go-Live Support:** Be the primary contact for troubleshooting and resolving any issues that arise after go-live.

By focusing on these areas, the solution architect ensures that the Microsoft Power Platform solution is successfully deployed and that the customer is well-equipped for the transition to the new system.

Conclusion

By combining the power of analytics, AI, and integration with structured ALM and go-live strategies, organizations can create innovative, scalable, and impactful Power Platform solutions. Analytics and AI enable data-driven decision-making and automation, while integration connects the platform with broader business systems. ALM and go-live strategies ensure that solutions are deployed efficiently and maintained for long-term success. As you implement these concepts, you'll transform your Power Platform projects into resilient and value-driven solutions.

CHAPTER 6

Assessing Your Expertise As a Microsoft Power Platform Solution Architect

Chapter Goal: To equip readers with the ability to apply their PL-600 knowledge in real-world business scenarios by analyzing, assessing, and providing solutions using Microsoft Power Platform and Dynamics 365. Through case studies and practical exercises, readers will refine their problem-solving skills and enhance their readiness for the certification exam.

Sub-topics:

1. Real-World Scenarios

CHAPTER 6 ASSESSING YOUR EXPERTISE AS A MICROSOFT POWER PLATFORM SOLUTION ARCHITECT

Introduction

Understanding real-world scenarios is key to becoming a successful solution architect. In this chapter, I have shared seven use case scenarios based on my experience in the manufacturing industry. These examples highlight common business challenges and how Power Platform and Dynamics 365 can solve them.

Each scenario will help you think critically, analyze problems, and design practical solutions using Power Apps, Power Automate, Power BI, and Dataverse. The goal is to not only test your knowledge but also improve your problem-solving skills.

As you go through these scenarios, try to relate them to your own industry or daily challenges. Think about how digital tools can improve efficiency, automate tasks, and enhance decision-making.

By the end of this chapter, you'll be better prepared to assess business problems, design effective solutions, and apply your skills in real-world projects. This hands-on approach will also help you succeed in the PL-600 exam and your career as a solution architect.

Case Study No. 1

Use Case: Leveraging Power Platform Components in a Real-World Apparel Manufacturing

Scenario

In an apparel manufacturing factory, the Sewing Line Production process involves multiple departments. These include Production, Quality, Industrial Engineering, Machine Maintenance, and Supermarkets (Fabric and Trims). Key performance indicators (KPIs) like efficiency, productivity, defect rates, downtime, and machine breakdowns are critical for daily management. They are also critical for decision-making. Manual reporting creates inefficiencies, delaying vital production decisions.

Goal

- To streamline production monitoring
- To enhance decision-making speed
- To remove manual report handling by leveraging Power Platform components (Power Apps, Power Automate, and Power BI)

Refer to Figure 6-1 for the step-by-step solution.

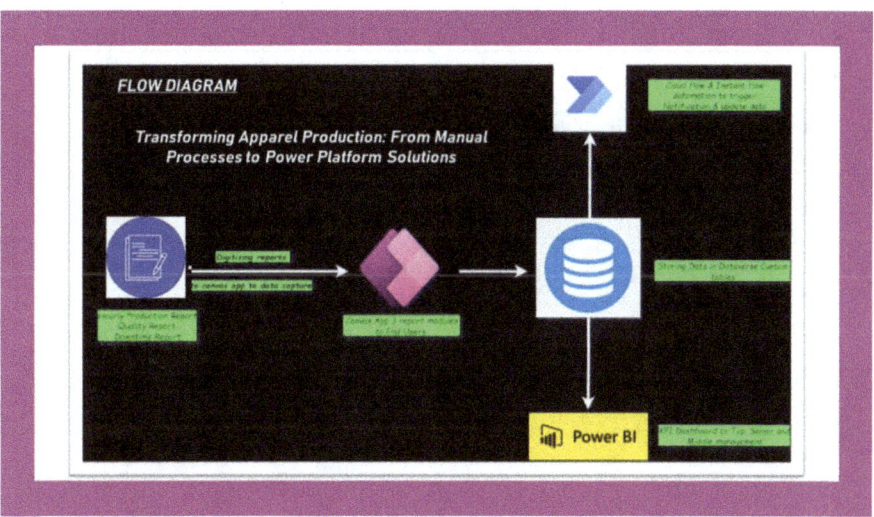

Figure 6-1. Sample Solution Flow Diagram

CHAPTER 6　ASSESSING YOUR EXPERTISE AS A MICROSOFT POWER PLATFORM SOLUTION ARCHITECT

1. Power Apps: Canvas App for Data Capture

Purpose: Replace manual paper-based hourly production monitoring with a digital solution that collects data in real time.

Development: Create a user-friendly Canvas app that supervisors can use to enter hourly production data directly from the sewing floor. The app allows them to

- Enter operator names, target output, actual output, and any issues like downtime or material shortages
- Store department-specific data like machine breakdowns or quality rejections in a single app
- Automate calculations for efficiency and productivity using predefined formulas

Benefits

- Eliminates time spent on manual reporting and reduces data entry errors.
- All production line data is stored in one place, accessible to middle management at any time.
- Supervisors no longer need to fill out multiple reports manually, making their tasks quicker and more efficient.

2. Power Automate: Automated Report Submission and Alerts

Purpose: Automatically inform managers about production issues and deliver reports in real time, speeding up decision-making.

Development: Set up an Instant Flow in Power Automate, triggered by a button in the Power App:

- **Hourly Alerts:** Supervisors can send the latest production status directly to management with a click. If certain thresholds (e.g., low productivity or high defect rates) are met, automatic notifications are sent to the concerned manager via email or Teams.

- **Bottleneck Alerts:** If a bottleneck is identified (e.g., machine downtime exceeding 30 minutes), the flow can automatically escalate the issue to senior management, ensuring faster responses.

Benefits

- Eliminates the need for supervisors to physically search for managers to report problems

- Ensures that bottlenecks are addressed promptly, minimizing production delays

- Automates the flow of real-time data for faster decision-making

3. Power BI: Real-Time Data Dashboards and KPI Monitoring

Purpose: Give management visual insights into production efficiency, bottlenecks, and overall performance using real-time data.

Development: Use Power BI to create dashboards that pull data from Dataverse (where the Canvas app stores the information) to visualize KPIs like

- Efficiency, productivity, defect rates, and downtime across different sewing lines

- Department-wise performance metrics (e.g., machine maintenance, quality control)

- Bottleneck analysis and production trends

Access

- Senior and top management can access these dashboards at any time to check factory performance.

- Historical data allows management to forecast production, find recurring issues, and improve processes.

Benefits

- Reduces the time needed to prepare reports, as the data is instantly available

- Allows management to track performance in real time and make informed decisions based on precise data

- Provides a holistic view of the factory's performance, integrating data from multiple departments

Outcome

By integrating Power Apps, Power Automate, and Power BI, the factory gains a real-time, automated production monitoring system. This solution minimizes manual work, accelerates decision-making, and improves overall efficiency, productivity, and accuracy in reporting.

Case Study No. 2
Digitizing Training School Processes with Microsoft Power Platform

In the modern apparel industry, efficiency and skill development play a pivotal role in maintaining a competitive edge. Let's assume there is a company called LK Garments. It operates in the manufacturing sector. The company sought to streamline and digitize its Training School process. This was to watch and enhance the efficiency of its Trainee-Operators and Trainers. The company used Microsoft Power Platform. It embarked on a journey to build a robust application. The application is for tracking training progress, efficiency, and outcomes.

Let's Understand the Requirement

The Training School at LK Garments (not a real company) had a clear set of requirements:

1. **Centralized Data Access:** Employee data were already available in the ERP system. This included name, age, gender, ID number, photo, fresher/experienced status, and operations. The skill matrices for experienced operators were also there. This needed integration.

2. **Diverse Training Methodologies**

    - **Freshers:** Focused on foundational skills, operations, and productivity

    - **Experienced Operators:** Upgraded specific skills based on gaps identified in the skill matrix

3. **Trainer KPI Tracking:** Metrics included

    - Number of trainees trained
    - Days taken to complete a trainee's training
    - Graduation percentage of trainees

4. **Trainee Performance Metrics:** Stages of training assessed based on

    - Quantity achieved
    - Quality of work
    - Efficiency in operations

Power Platform Components

1. Power Apps

A user-friendly interface was developed to capture and manage training data. The application featured

- **Integration with ERP:** Using Microsoft Dataverse to pull employee data directly from the existing ERP system.
- **Role-Based Access:** Trainers input trainee performance data, while managers accessed consolidated views.
- **Training Modules:** Separate workflows for freshers and experienced operators with respective SOPs and KPIs.

2. Power Automate

Automation ensured a seamless flow of data and notifications:

- **Daily Reporting:** Trainers received automated reminders to input trainee progress.

- **Approval Workflows:** Training completion requests were routed to supervisors for validation.

- **Skill Gap Alerts:** Notifications were sent for operators requiring further upskilling based on training outcomes to IE and HR Team.

3. Power BI

A dynamic dashboard visualized training progress and efficiency metrics:

- **Trainee Performance:** Quantity, quality, and efficiency trends over time

- **Trainer KPIs:** Number of trainees trained, average training time, and graduation rates

- **Comparative Analysis:** Benchmarking between trainers and across batches

Benefits

1. **Increased Transparency:** Real-time data on training progress enhanced decision-making.

2. **Enhanced Efficiency:** Trainers could focus on skill development while automation handled repetitive tasks.

3. **Improved Trainee Outcomes:** Performance metrics highlighted areas of improvement, ensuring tailored training.

4. **Data-Driven Insights:** Power BI provided actionable intelligence to improve training methodologies.

Takeaways

Digitizing the Training School process using Microsoft Power Platform brought about a significant change. It revolutionized how LK Garments (not a real company) managed skill development. It also enhanced the monitoring process. By integrating ERP data, automating workflows, and visualizing insights, the solution bridged operational gaps and empowered stakeholders with real-time information.

This project serves as a model for leveraging technology to enhance training efficiency in the manufacturing industry. The fusion of Power Apps, Power Automate, and Power BI demonstrates the platform's versatility in solving complex business challenges.

Case Study No. 3
Transforming E-Commerce Operations with Microsoft Power Platform

Small garment businesses often face challenges in expanding their customer base. They also struggle with streamlining sales processes and managing operations without incurring high costs. Microsoft Power Platform provides an affordable, scalable, and easy-to-implement solution to create an end-to-end e-commerce platform tailored to your needs.

In this case study, we'll explore how small garment companies can use Power Platform to create an e-commerce solution. This solution simplifies online sales and operations. It also enhances customer satisfaction.

Why Power Platform for E-Commerce?

Power Apps, **Power Automate**, **Power BI**, and **Dataverse** are all part of Microsoft Power Platform. They combine to create low-code applications. These applications integrate seamlessly with existing tools like Microsoft 365 and Dynamics 365. This platform enables small businesses to

- Build customizable e-commerce solutions
- Automate sales and inventory workflows
- Gain actionable insights to improve customer engagement and sales

Core Components of a Power Platform E-Commerce Solution

1. Customer-Facing E-Commerce App (Power Apps)

Use Power Apps to build a mobile-friendly e-commerce platform where customers can

- Browse garments with images, sizes, and prices
- Add products to their cart and place orders
- Track order status and shipping updates

CHAPTER 6   ASSESSING YOUR EXPERTISE AS A MICROSOFT POWER PLATFORM SOLUTION ARCHITECT

Features

- **Product Catalog:** Showcase your garments with categories, descriptions, and availability.

- **Dynamic Pricing:** Update prices easily without coding.

- **Customer Profiles:** Allow customers to create accounts for faster checkout.

2. Inventory Management System (Power Automate + Dataverse)

Integrate Dataverse to store product data and Power Automate to manage inventory workflows:

- Automate inventory updates when products are sold.

- Notify admins about low stock levels.

- Sync inventory data with suppliers or warehouses.

3. Order Management Workflow (Power Automate)

Streamline order processing with automated workflows:

- Trigger order confirmation emails after payment.

- Generate invoices automatically and store them in OneDrive or SharePoint.

- Notify the dispatch team with customer details and product specifications.

4. Analytics Dashboard (Power BI)

Create a Power BI dashboard to track key e-commerce metrics, including

- Sales performance by category, product, or region
- Customer behavior and purchase patterns
- Profitability and inventory turnover rates

These insights enable you to make data-driven decisions and refine your business strategy.

5. Customer Support Chatbot (Power Virtual Agents)

Offer 24/7 customer support with Power Virtual Agents:

- Assist customers in finding products or placing orders.
- Provide updates on order status or return policies.
- Escalate complex queries to human agents via email or Microsoft Teams.

Step-by-Step Implementation Plan

1. **Set Up the Product Database**

    Use Dataverse to store garment details like product names, sizes, prices, and images.

2. **Build the Customer App**

    - Use Power Apps to create a user-friendly interface for browsing and purchasing garments.
    - Customize the app with branding, categories, and payment integration (e.g., Stripe or PayPal).

3. **Automate Inventory and Order Workflows**

    - Use Power Automate to connect the app to Dataverse and automate inventory updates.

    - Set up email notifications for customers and admin teams.

4. **Design an Analytics Dashboard**

    - Use Power BI to pull data from Dataverse and visualize sales performance and customer behavior.

5. **Deploy and Optimize**

    - Test the app with a small group of customers and gather feedback.

    - Optimize based on user feedback and launch the app to a wider audience.

Benefits for Small Garment Companies

1. **Cost-Effective**

    Power Platform eliminates the need for expensive third-party e-commerce platforms by providing a low-code, in-house solution.

2. **Customization**

    Tailor the platform to match your business's unique needs, such as garment categories, pricing models, and workflows.

CHAPTER 6   ASSESSING YOUR EXPERTISE AS A MICROSOFT POWER PLATFORM SOLUTION ARCHITECT

3. **Scalability**

    Easily add features like bulk order processing, discount codes, or loyalty programs as your business grows.

4. **Real-Time Insights**

    Use Power BI to track performance and optimize operations based on data trends.

5. **Quick Deployment**

    With Power Platform, you can build and launch your e-commerce solution in weeks rather than months.

Real-World Example: Transforming a Small Garment Business

A small garment company used Power Platform to create a custom e-commerce app for their local market. By integrating inventory management, order workflows, and analytics, they reduced manual effort by 60%.

Case Study No. 4
Maximize Compliance: Self-Assessments and Audits with Power Platform

Garment manufacturers and suppliers are required to implement customer or brand policies, procedures, and certifications that focus on social, safety, environmental, and quality standards to secure orders. These policies often include

- Conducting self-assessments based on buyer policies and procedures

- Hosting buyer or certification body audits

- Maintaining a cycle of yearly audits to retain certifications and meet compliance standards

Internal audits have become increasingly important to maintain good scores with buyers and certification bodies. Conducted every two to three months, these audits help ensure that documents are up to date and standards are consistently met.

Who Conducts the Audits?

- **Self-Assessments:** Performed by safety officers, welfare officers, compliance officers, or middle management

- **Internal Audits:** Carried out by senior management, internal auditors, or compliance managers

In this case study, we will explore how to build an efficient system for self-assessments and internal audits using **Microsoft Power Platform**, leveraging its components—Power Apps, Power Automate, and Power BI—for seamless data management, automation, and reporting.

Creating an Assessment and Auditing System Using Power Platform

Why Use Power Platform?

Microsoft Power Platform provides a low-code environment to

- **Build Custom Apps (Power Apps):** Simplify self-assessments and audits with easy-to-use interfaces.

- **Automate Notifications and Workflows (Power Automate):** Ensure timely reminders and escalations.

- **Visualize Data (Power BI):** Gain actionable insights through interactive dashboards.

This approach ensures scalability, flexibility, and integration with existing Microsoft 365 tools.

Define the Assessment and Audit Process

1. Employees perform a **self-assessment** based on buyer or brand requirements.

2. Internal auditors review the same criteria and document their findings.

3. A centralized system stores all data for analysis and follow-up actions.

Build the Self-Assessment App in Power Apps

1. **Create a Canvas App**

   - Open Power Apps and select **Canvas App**.

   - Design a user-friendly form interface for employees to fill out their self-assessments.

2. **Design the Form**

   - Include controls like drop-downs, toggles, text inputs, and ratings.

   - Group questions into categories such as Safety, Compliance, and Quality.

3. **Connect to a Data Source**

    - Store responses in Dataverse, SharePoint, or Excel.

    - Set up a table or list to capture employee names, responses, and timestamps.

4. **Publish and Share**

    - Publish the app and share it with employees for self-assessment submissions.

Create an Internal Audit App for Auditors

1. **Duplicate the Self-Assessment App**

    - Copy the Canvas App and modify it for internal audit use.

2. **Enhance with Audit-Specific Features**

    - Add fields for auditor comments, scores, and "Audit Status" (Pass/Fail).

    - Include filtering options to review completed self-assessments.

3. **Role-Based Security**

    - Implement role-based security in Dataverse to restrict access appropriately for auditors and employees.

Automate Notifications and Workflows with Power Automate

1. **Send Reminders**
   - Create a flow to send periodic email reminders for completing self-assessments.

2. **Notify Auditors**
   - Trigger notifications to internal auditors when a self-assessment is submitted.

3. **Escalation Workflow**
   - Escalate incomplete assessments or unresolved audit findings to supervisors.

Visualize Data with Power BI

1. **Connect to the Data Source**
   - Use Power BI to connect to Dataverse or SharePoint lists.

2. **Create Dashboards**
   - Track key metrics, such as
     - Self-assessment completion rates
     - Internal audit scores by department or category
     - Trends over time

3. **Embed Reports**
   - Share dashboards via Teams or SharePoint for stakeholders to access insights easily.

Iterate and Improve

Gather feedback from employees and auditors to refine the system. Regularly update forms, workflows, and reports to address changing requirements and enhance user experience.

Benefits of Power Platform for Compliance and Technical Auditing

1. **Centralized Data Management:** Store all responses securely in one location.

2. **Automation:** Reduce manual effort with automated workflows and reminders.

3. **Real-Time Insights:** Monitor performance and compliance trends through dashboards.

4. **Scalability:** Adapt the system for different departments or industry standards.

Case Study No. 5
Transform Vendor Evaluation with Power Platform

Let's first understand what vendor evaluation is. Before diving into the specifics of how the Power Platform can transform vendor evaluation, it's important to know why it's so important.

In today's highly competitive business environment, companies rely on a vast network of vendors. These vendors supply products and services that are critical to their operations. But not all vendors deliver the same level of quality, cost-efficiency, or reliability. Vendor evaluation is a process. Businesses assess their vendors based on key factors like price. They also consider product quality, on-time delivery, customer support, and safety measures.

Effective vendor evaluation helps businesses choose partners that align with their operational goals and standards. It ensures that they keep high-quality products. They meet delivery timelines. They also keep costs under control. All of these factors are essential for maintaining a competitive edge in the marketplace. But as businesses grow, the manual management of vendor evaluation data becomes time-consuming and prone to error. This is where the Power Platform comes in. It offers a digital solution to automate, streamline, and enhance the vendor evaluation process.

Evaluation Criteria

These criteria are not only used to evaluate the vendors; based on business requirements, they are liable to change.

- **Price:** Evaluating the cost-effectiveness of the vendor's offerings compared to others in the market. Price should show the value delivered without compromising quality.

- **Quality of Product:** Assessing the consistency and standards of the products provided. We confirm they meet required specifications. This prevents production issues.

- **On-Time Delivery:** It measures the vendor's reliability in delivering goods within the agreed timeline. This is crucial for maintaining smooth operations and avoiding delays.

- **Customer Support:** Evaluating the responsiveness and helpfulness of the vendor's customer service team in resolving issues or answering queries promptly.

- **Material Commuting Cost:** Analyze the cost of transporting materials. Consider the distance from the vendor's location to your facility. Include logistics and other transportation-related expenses.

- **Safety Measures:** The vendor must follow necessary safety protocols during production. This ensures safety during transportation. These measures reduce the risk of accidents, product defects, or compliance violations.

- **Goods Return:** Monitoring how often products are returned due to defects or incorrect deliveries. Evaluating how quickly and easily the vendor resolves these issues is also important. A high number of returns or slow resolution can affect your operations, so it's important to check this closely.

Use Case

To understand the evaluation process, we will take an example company called LK Fashion. This is not a real company. LK Fashion wants to implement a vendor evaluation process as part of its buyer requirements. LK Fashion's management has decided to design the solution in-house instead of purchasing readily available products.

CHAPTER 6 ASSESSING YOUR EXPERTISE AS A MICROSOFT POWER PLATFORM SOLUTION ARCHITECT

Let's Help LK Fashion to Gather Data for Vendor Evaluation

Data Source for Vendor Evaluation

- **Price:** Extract from the invoice linked to each purchase order–ERP.

- **Quality of Product:** Gather from the inspection report conducted upon goods receipt, based on the purchase order–Manual Report.

- **On-Time Delivery:** Compare the product in-housing date with the expected delivery date on the purchase order–ERP.

- **Customer Support:** Use data from a ticket-raising email that logs support issues and their resolution–not a formatted Mail.

- **Material Commuting Cost:** Record from the transportation or logistics cost mentioned in the invoice–ERP.

- **Safety Measures:** Obtain from audits conducted on the vendor's workplace and adherence to safety SOPs–Manual Report.

- **Goods Return:** Collect from the return shipment records, including reasons for the return (e.g., defective or incorrect items)–ERP.

CHAPTER 6　ASSESSING YOUR EXPERTISE AS A MICROSOFT POWER PLATFORM SOLUTION ARCHITECT

Let's Deep Dive into the Solution

Manual Reports to Power Application

As LK Fashion already has available data except for manual reports like the Safety Measures audit report, Inspection report, and Customer Support mail:

- **Safety Measures Report:** Managed by auditors
- **Inspection Report:** Handled by QA and QC in the warehouse and store
- **Customer Support:** Managed by Sourcing Executives

we will digitize the manual reports into a Power Application. Specifically, we will use a Canvas App that includes photo capturing facilities. This will document audit failure points, inspection approvals, and customer support evidence. Data will be stored in customized Dataverse tables with business rules and calculation fields to fulfill the requirements.

SQL Data Modeling

LK Fashion has other data like price, on-time delivery, extra costs, and goods return in the ERP. We will integrate this data using a SQL intermediate table. This will build a common data model with primary keys and mandatory required fields. We need these for evaluation as source data is available in multiple tables. A daily scheduled job queue will load the data into the SQL destination table.

Power BI Dashboard and Report

Once the source data is ready, we'll connect the SQL and Dataverse destination tables to Power BI Desktop. We will transform and clean the data if required. Then, we will create the reports.

Building the Dashboard

- **Import Data:** Load the integrated data from both SQL and Dataverse into Power BI.

- **Transform Data:** Use Power Query Editor for any necessary data transformation (removing unnecessary columns, creating calculated columns, etc.).

- **Create Relationships:** Set up relationships between tables to guarantee precise data analysis.

- **Design Visuals:** Add various visualizations (bar charts, line graphs, tables) to represent the evaluation criteria and key performance indicators.

- **Add Interactivity:** Implement filters, slicers, and drill-through capabilities for an interactive user experience.

- **Publish the Dashboard:** Once the dashboard is complete, publish it to the Power BI Service for sharing with stakeholders.

Automation Features

- **Scheduled Refresh:** Set up a scheduled refresh in Power BI Service to keep the data up-to-date automatically.

- **Alerts and Notifications:** Create alerts for key metrics (e.g., if on-time delivery drops below a certain threshold) to guarantee prompt responses to issues.

- **User Access Control:** Manage user permissions and access levels in the Power BI Service. This ensures sensitive data is only available to authorized personnel.

Case Study No. 6
Bridging Skill Gaps in Apparel Production Using Power Platform Tools
Apparel Production Skill Gap Overview

In the apparel industry, line production is a method where the garment-making process is broken into smaller steps. Each worker or machine is responsible for one step, like stitching a sleeve or attaching buttons. The garment moves from one worker to the next until it's finished. This system helps make clothes faster and in large quantities. It also makes it easier to check for quality at each step.

One major challenge in line production in the apparel industry is managing the absenteeism and attrition of skilled workers. This often happens without prior notice. This issue is compounded by a shortage of skilled workers in the industry. The industry operates based on strict time requirements. It also has efficiency requirements. Daily production targets are set for an eight-hour workday (480 minutes).

Each worker's target is determined by the Standard Allowed Minutes (SAM) for each task. The SAM is calculated based on the cycle time in seconds and other factors. This system highlights the critical importance of time in apparel production. Meeting production goals relies on having enough skilled workers who can complete their tasks efficiently within the set time limits.

Now let's dive into the solution using Power Platform components.

Solution Overview: Addressing Absenteeism

Background: LK Fashions (not a real company) operates 25 production lines and plans to expand by adding 10 new lines. However, the factory faces challenges with absenteeism and attrition, impacting the efficiency and productivity of the production lines.

Challenges

- **Absenteeism:** Uninformed leaves disrupt production and reduce efficiency. Despite awareness training, employees continue to take uninformed leaves.

- **Attrition:** The lack of skilled operators for the new production lines due to high attrition rates.

Data Required

- **Daily Absenteeism Data:** Information on who is absent, including reasons for absence

- **Existing Workers Skill Matrix:** Current skills and qualifications of the existing workforce

- **Fixed Operators:** List of fixed operators in the production line if company follows.

Proposed Solution

1. **Capturing Absenteeism Data**
    - **Method:** Implement an IVR (Interactive Voice Response) system for capturing absenteeism data. Employees can call in and record their absenteeism using an automated phone system.

- **Technology:** Utilize Azure Communication Services to build the IVR system. This service offers integration, scalability, flexibility, and cost-effectiveness.

2. **Storing Absenteeism Data**

    - **Storage:** Use Microsoft Dataverse to store the absenteeism data.

    - **Data Capture:** The IVR system captures data like the dialed phone number, entry reason for leave, and timestamp.

    - **Integration:** Power Automate will trigger a flow. This flow will add records to the Dataverse table. This happens whenever new IVR call data is received.

    Example Data Table

    - **PhoneNumber:** Text

    - **LeaveReason:** Text

    - **Timestamp:** DateTime

3. **Notification and Data Utilization**

    Notification to HR and IE Departments

    - **Timing:** Set up a Power Automate scheduled flow. This flow will send an email to the HR and Industrial Engineering (IE) departments. The email will be sent every morning at 8:45 AM.

    - **Content:** The email will include the list of uninformed absences. It will provide the HR and IE teams with the information needed to address absenteeism. This helps them make decisions to mitigate productivity loss.

Benefits

- **Efficiency:** Automated data capture reduces manual entry and errors, improving the accuracy of absenteeism records.

- **Timeliness:** Daily email notifications give HR and IE departments timely information to take necessary actions before the production day starts.

- **Scalability:** The IVR system and Dataverse integration are scalable to handle increasing data volume as the factory expands.

Case Study No. 7

Bridging Skill Gaps: Leveraging Power Platform for Production Line Expansion and Attrition

In this case study, we explore how **LK Fashions** (not a real company) leverages **Power BI** and **Power Automate**. They address challenges related to **worker attrition** and **skill shortages**. These issues arise as they expand their production lines for new styles. By taking a data-driven approach, LK Fashions ensures they can meet operational demands while maintaining efficiency.

Data Requirements

To address the **skill gap** challenge, LK Fashions integrates and monitors the following data:

- **New Styles Skill Matrix:** Captures the required skills for new styles based on incoming orders
- **Existing Operators' Skills Matrix:** Tracks current skill levels across production lines
- **Attrition Data:** Daily updates on operator turnover

Operators' Skill Matrix Management

Existing Operators' Skill Matrix

The **Industrial Engineering (IE) team** maintains a skill matrix in Excel that is updated monthly. This matrix provides an up-to-date view of operators' skills across production lines to ensure operational needs are met.

New Styles Operators' Skill Matrix

The production lines are expanding due to a large order from buyer XYZ. LK Fashions is preparing to meet new style demands within three months. The **IE team** updates the matrix with the skills required for the new styles to assess gaps and plan accordingly.

Attrition Data Management

The **HR department** follows a strict **Standard Operating Procedure (SOP)** to monitor attrition rates. They update the attrition data daily to provide real-time insight into staff turnover and how it affects production capacity.

Data Integration and Automation

Power Automate Workflow

- The **existing operator skill matrix** and **new style skill requirements** Excel files are uploaded daily into Power BI. This is done using **Power Automate**.

- This automated process eliminates manual effort, ensuring that Power BI always uses the latest data for analysis.

KPI Monitoring

A **Quality Management System (QMS)** has been implemented at LK Fashions to monitor key performance indicators (KPIs) across departments:

- **HR Department KPIs:** Absenteeism %, Uninformed leave %, Attrition %, and Recruitment process

- **IE Department KPIs:** Operator skill improvement and training process effectiveness

Power BI Dashboard for Management

Using **Power BI**, LK Fashions has developed a **management dashboard** that includes multiple reports based on departmental KPIs. These reports are updated daily. Middle, senior, and top management consume them to support long-term planning. They also use them to forecast skill gap solutions.

Example Scenario

For the **T-shirt Side Seam Operation**:

- **Existing Skill Matrix:** 100 operators are required.
- **Available Operators:** 99 operators.
- **New Skill Requirement Due to Attrition:** 1 operator.
- **New Skill Requirement Due to Production Line Expansion:** 20 operators.

This analysis helps management make informed decisions on

- Hiring new operators
- Allocating training resources
- Reallocating current workforce across production lines

Scheduled Alerts and Real-Time Decision-Making

Using **Power BI** and **Power Automate**, LK Fashions has set up scheduled alerts to notify relevant managers and department heads when abnormal KPIs are detected (e.g., high absenteeism or attrition rates). These alerts provide

- **Recruitment and Training Plans:** Notifications trigger when recruitment or training needs arise due to operator shortages or skill gaps.
- **Attrition and Absenteeism Management:** Alerts ensure that the management team can take timely decisions to mitigate workforce shortages.

By integrating **real-time alerts**, LK Fashions can quickly address operational challenges. They can also ensure continuity in production as they expand their capacity.

This automated system ensures that LK Fashions can effectively monitor key metrics. It allows them to respond to skill gap issues in real time. This leads to sustained operational efficiency and long-term success.

Conclusion

Real-world scenarios are the true test of a solution architect's skills. In this chapter, you explored seven practical use cases from the manufacturing industry and learned how to apply Power Platform and Dynamics 365 to solve business challenges. These scenarios helped you analyze problems, define requirements, and design effective solutions.

By working through these cases, you've strengthened your ability to think critically and approach business problems with a solution-oriented mindset. Now, take this a step further—identify challenges in your own industry or daily work, and try to develop solutions using the skills you've learned.

Mastering real-world application is what sets apart a great solution architect. Keep practicing, keep refining your approach, and you'll be well-prepared for both the PL-600 certification and real-world projects.

Index

A

Agents, 197
AI, *see* Artificial Intelligence (AI)
AI Builder, 261
Apparel manufacturing factory, case study
    automated report submission/alerts, 294, 295
    manual reporting, 293
    Power apps, 294
    Power BI, 295, 296
Apparel production skill gap
    absenteeism, 317
    benefits, 319
    challenge, 316
    proposed solution, 317, 318
Application Lifecycle Management (ALM), 188, 247, 248
    Azure DevOps, 280
    deployment methodologies, pipeline, 282, 283
    go-live phase, solution deployment, 283–290
    Microsoft vision, 274, 275
    pipelines, 281, 282
    solution architects, 275
    solutions, 274, 276
        characteristics, 276
        layering, 277, 278
        rules for creating, 279
        splitting approaches, 279, 280
        strategies, 278
        types, 277
AppSource, 98, 99
Artificial Intelligence (AI)
    AI Builder, 261
    Azure cognitive services, 260
    Azure machine learning, 261
    choosing appropriate AI solution, 262
    definition, 259
    Dynamics 365 apps, 260
    OpenAI, 260
Azure, 26, 42
Azure Bot framework, 202, 208
Azure Bot Service, 202
Azure Cognitive Services, 260
Azure Data Lake, 224, 227
Azure DevOps, 28, 280
Azure Machine Learning, 261
Azure Monitor, 152
Azure virtual machines, 194

INDEX

B

Bot Framework Composer, 203
BPFs, *see* Business process flows (BPFs)
Business process flows (BPFs), 175

C

Canvas apps, 149
CD, *see* Continuous Deployment (CD)
CDM, *see* Common Data Model (CDM)
CI, *see* Continuous Integration (CI)
Common Data Model (CDM), 97, 212
    benefits, 216
    data architecture, 217
    data models, types, 217, 218
    definition, 213
    ERDs, 219
    features, 213, 214
    Microsoft industry accelerators, 215, 216
    object diagrams, 219
Connectors, 225, 227
Continuous Deployment (CD), 280
Continuous Integration (CI), 280
Customer discovery
    communication strategy
        active listening/empathy, 49
        collaborative tools, 50, 51
        feedback/iteration, 51
        initial contact/relationship building, 48
        long-term relationships, 52
        requirements, 50
        stakeholders, 49
        success criteria, 51
        transparency, 49
    customer and design, 43
    discovery meetings, 47
    initial process, 45
    interviews, 44
    LK Tech solutions, 46, 47, 53
    meetings, 44
Customer Service Hub, 144

D

Data Loss Prevention (DLP), 232
Data modeling and security
    CDM, 212
    data store, 222–227
    dataverse, 235
    environment security, 228
    factors, 221, 222
    Microsoft Entra ID
        authentication, 228–230
    roles/administration, 231–235
    security apps, 241–245
    security groups/environment access, 231
    solution architect, 210–212
    strategies, 220
    virtual tables, 226, 227

Dataverse, 223, 227, 250, 292
 auditing, 241
 benefits, 124, 125
 business units, 239
 cloud deployments, 119, 120
 column-level security, 240
 compliance/data
  protection, 121
 custom logic, 127–130
 data accessing/storing, 123, 124
 data residency, 120
 design, 130
 design principles, 237
 environment data location, 119
 environments, 115, 116
 extensibility/customization,
  125, 126
 hierarchical security, 240
 landing zones, 122
 managed environments,
  121, 122
 multiple environments, 117, 121
 on-premises systems, 122
 security architecture, 235
 security design, 236
 security features, 238
 security layers, 118, 119
 security roles, 239
 table ownership, 238, 239
 tenants, 116
Digitizing training school process
 LK Garments, 297, 298
 Power platform
  components, 298–300
DLP, *see* Data Loss
  Prevention (DLP)
Dynamics 365 apps, 24, 26, 28, 42,
  97, 99, 141, 179, 301

E

E-commerce, case study
 components, 301–303
 implementation, 303, 304
 sales and operations, 301
 small garment companies,
  benefits, 304, 305
Entity Relationship Diagrams
 (ERDs), 217, 219
ERDs, *see* Entity Relationship
  Diagrams (ERDs)

F, G, H

Fit-gap analysis, 33, 90, 91,
  93, 95, 99

I, J

Independent software vendors
 (ISVs), 28, 67
Integration
 challenges, 263, 264, 267
 data categories, 272, 273
 definition, 262
 design, 268, 269, 271, 272
 design resilience, 271
 failures, 269, 270

INDEX

Integration (*cont.*)
    solution architects, 265, 266
    types, 264, 265
Interactive Voice Response (IVR)
    system, 317
ISVs, *see* Independent software
    vendors (ISVs)
IVR system, *see* Interactive Voice
    Response (IVR) system

K

Key performance indicators
    (KPIs), 39, 292
KPIs, *see* Key performance
    indicators (KPIs)

L

Language Understanding (LUIS)
    service, 206
Logical data model, 218
LUIS service, *see* Language
    Understanding
    (LUIS) service

M

MFA, *see* Multifactor
    Authentication (MFA)
Microsoft 365, 26, 42, 114, 301
Microsoft 365 Copilot license, 201
Microsoft Copilot Studio
    agent building options, 202–205

AI principles, 201
building agents, 206–210
building agents,
    challenges, 197
conversational AI, 197
language processing, 198
solution architect, deploying
    agents, 200, 201
use cases, agents, 198, 199
Microsoft Dataverse, 115
Microsoft Dynamics 365, 251
Microsoft Entra ID tenant, 116
Microsoft Learn, 5, 7, 12, 20, 22
Microsoft Power Platform,
    3, 24, 26, 222
    API calls, 134
    API requests, 131
    capabilities, 114
    components, 112, 113
    data, 115
    dataverse, 115
    entitlement limits, 132
    high availability, 134
    high availability/disaster
        recovery
        mechanisms, 135–139
    project governance, 102, 103
        checkpoints, 111
        deliver bad news, 107
        experience, 105
        feedback, 107
        project failure, 109
        retrospectives, 111
        review work, 108

INDEX

risks, 105
solution architects, 103, 104, 106
successful projects, characteristics, 110
retry policies/patterns, 133
service limits, 132, 133
Multifactor Authentication (MFA), 229

N

Natural Language Processing (NLP), 206
NLP, *see* Natural Language Processing (NLP)

O

Outlook, 167

P

PAD, *see* Power Automate Desktop (PAD)
Physical data models, 218
PL-600 exam
　architecting solution, 4
　business process requirements, 4
　ESL accommodation, 8–11
　exam preparation, 5–8
　exam room requirement, 21
　implementing solution, 4
　Microsoft exam structure and format
　　build lists, 18
　　case studies, 17
　　inline choice, 19, 20
　　lab simulations, 19
　　multiple choice, 17, 18
　　question series, 17
　　scenario-based questions, 19
　　true/false, 19
　practical preparation strategies, 1
　register for exam
　　Microsoft Learn account, 11
　　personal email, 12–14
　　reshedule, 16
　　system check, 14, 15
　　time management, 20, 21
PoC, *see* Proof of concept (PoC)
Portal apps, 141
Power Apps, 97, 292
　app type, 142–144
　Canvas apps, 148–151
　components, 146–148
　custom applications, 140
　extending existing apps *vs.* creation new, 144, 145
　Microsoft Apps *vs.* Partner Apps *vs.* Dynamics 365, 141, 142
　Microsoft Teams, 153–155
　monitoring/testing tools, Canvas apps, 151–153
　portals, 157–161
　types, 140, 141

329

INDEX

Power Automate, 2, 97, 183, 292
    BPFs, 175–179
    customer logic options, 161
        business rules, 162
        classic workflows, 163
        cloud flows, 164
        connectors, 165
        cost, 166
        dataverse
          connector, 170–175
        desktop flows, 165
        plug-ins, 163, 164
        triggers, 166–169
Power Automate Desktop (PAD), 187
Power BI, 2, 97, 292
Power Pages, 113
Power Platform, 26, 42, 97, 99
Power Platform Developer Associate (PL-400), 2
Power Platform Functional Consultant (PL-200), 2
Power Platform—Power Apps, 2
Process mining, 194
Proof of concept (PoC), 93

Q

QMS, *see* Quality Management System (QMS)
Quality Management System (QMS), 321

R

Reporting and analytics
    AI, 253
    alternative reporting options, 258, 259
    export data to excel, 256
    Microsoft Dynamics 365, 251, 252
    model-driven apps, 254–256
    report wizard, 257, 258
    requirements, 249
    solution architect role, 249, 250
    solution architects, 252, 253
    types, 250, 251
    Word and Excel templates, 257
Request for Proposal (RFP), 45
RFP, *see* Request for Proposal (RFP)
Robotic Process Automation (RPA), 165
    AI-driven assistance, 181
    browser requirements, 188
    data modeling, 182
    deployment/IT coordination, 187
    designing flows, 185, 186
    desktop flows
        runnning, 192, 193
        variables, 191
    desktop flows, Power Automate, 186, 187
    legacy systems, 183
    Microsoft Power Platform, 188

INDEX

Power Automate, 183, 184
process mining, 194–196
record/edit tasks, 189–191
solution architect, 184, 185
solutions/ALM, 188, 189
user's actions, 183
virtual machines, unattended flows, 193, 194
RPA, *see* Robotic Process Automation (RPA)

S

Sales Hub, 144
SAM, *see* Standard Allowed Minutes (SAM)
Self-assessments and audits, case study
benefits, 310
creating assessments, 306–309
policies, 305
Single Sign-On (SSO), 228
Skill gaps, LK fashions
data integration/automation, 321
data requirements, 320
KPI monitoring, 321
operators skill matrix, 320
Power BI management dashboard, 321, 322
scheduled alerts/real-time decision-making, 322, 323
SMEs, *see* Subject matter experts (SMEs)

Software-as-a-Service (SaaS) solution, 114
Solution architect, 184
analysis/design, 32, 33
assessing/refining requirements
AppSource, 98, 99
connectors/APIs, 97
feasibility, 90–93
fit-gap analysis, 90
fit-gap analysis/business requirements, 95, 96
industry acclerators/CDM, 97, 98
PoC, 93, 94
business application
availability/recoverability, 38, 39
compliance/privacy, 37
design/trade-offs, 41, 42
efficiency/operations, 40
empowerment, 36, 37
maintenance, 38
performance/scalability, 39
security, 35, 36
shared responsibility, 40, 41
customer discovery, 100
customer discovery essentials, 23, 24
delivery, project, 34
develop/validate demo, 63–65
functional and nonfunctional requirements, 75
acceptance criteria, 80, 81
capture exceptions, 81

331

INDEX

Solution architect (*cont.*)
    conflicting requirements, 78
    example, 79
    feasibility, 77, 85, 86
    finalizing requirement, 89, 90
    managing attendees, 77
    mapping process, 80
    poorly worded requirements, 79
    prework, 77
    prioritization, 76
    requirement capture sessions, 75
    review process, 86–88
    scope creep, 81
    types, 82–85
  implementation, 33, 34
  ISV, 67–69
  licensing, 69
  manage expectations, 66
  operation, project, 34
  PoC, 65
  presales, 31, 32
  project initiation, 32
  proposed solution, 59–62
  soft skills, 25
  soft skills, C's, 5, 29, 30
  solution envisioning, 24
  stakeholders, 53
  strength/weakness, 70–74
  structured approach
    customization *vs.* extension, 54, 55
    design/proof of concept, 54
    documenting requirements, 55, 56
    identifying solution components, 56
    strengths and weaknesses, 58
    third party components, 58
    validating PoC, 57
  technologies, 26, 28
  third-party components, 66
SOP, *see* Standard Operating Procedure (SOP)
SQL Server Reporting Services (SSRS), 257, 258
SQL Server Transparent Data Encryption (TDE), 119
SSO, *see* Single Sign-On (SSO)
SSRS, *see* SQL Server Reporting Services (SSRS)
Standard Allowed Minutes (SAM), 316
Standard Operating Procedure (SOP), 320
Subject matter experts (SMEs), 198, 204

T

Triggers, 166
Twitter, 167

INDEX

U

Unique selling points (USPs), 72
USPs, *see* Unique selling points (USPs)

V, W, X, Y, Z

Vendor evaluation, case study
  business environment, 310
  business requirements, 311, 312
  Power BI dashboard and report, 315, 316
  SQL data modeling, 314
  use case, 312–314
Virtual Machines (VMs), 194
Virtual tables, 226, 227
Visual Studio, 258
VMs, *see* Virtual Machines (VMs)

333

GPSR Compliance

The European Union's (EU) General Product Safety Regulation (GPSR) is a set of rules that requires consumer products to be safe and our obligations to ensure this.

If you have any concerns about our products, you can contact us on

ProductSafety@springernature.com

In case Publisher is established outside the EU, the EU authorized representative is:

Springer Nature Customer Service Center GmbH
Europaplatz 3
69115 Heidelberg, Germany

www.ingramcontent.com/pod-product-compliance
Lightning Source LLC
LaVergne TN
LVHW010335260326
834688LV00036B/716